THE PRAXIS OF SERVANT
A guide for creating p... leaders through EDBI

EDBI is a process for developing servant leaders who lift others and inspire a spirit of generative servant leadership in the communities where they live and work by doing the following:

- ➢ **Embracing** self-awareness and self-identity
- ➢ **Developing** biblically based character
- ➢ **Building** capacity to serve
- ➢ **Inspiring** others to serve

STANFORD E. ANGION

CONTENTS

Upfront
Introduction

The Praxis of Procreant Servant Leadership
Chapter 1

A Deeper Dive into the "Leadership" of Procreant Servant Leadership
Chapter 2

The Supreme Model for Procreant Servant Leadership
Chapter 3

Embracing Self-Awareness and Self-Identity
Chapter 4

Developing Biblically-Based Character
Chapter 5

Building Capacity to Serve
Chapter 6

Inspiring Others to Serve
Chapter 7

Lifting Our Communities
Chapter 8

Acknowledgements

I am deeply grateful to my wife, Athenia; and daughters, Ivana and Kendra, for the love and support that they have given me over the years. Also, I am deeply thankful to Mt. Gilead Baptist Church, Selma University, and other relationships and institutional experiences that have helped to shape my understanding about Procreant Servant Leadership.

Much thanks to Dr. McArthur Floyd, Dr. Oscar Montgomery, and Stacy K for reading and providing feedback for this book.

Most of all, I truly thank God for the revelation and wherewithal to practice and capture these thoughts about Procreant Servant Leadership in this book.

UPFRONT!!!
Perfecting and Projecting Healing and Strength

My own brokenness, which has been my greatest impediment to lifting and leading others, has been my greatest asset for perfecting and projecting healing and strength in myself and those among whom I live and work.

Henri Nouman, in *The Wounded Healer*, talks about a healer who spends time wrapping his own wounds so he will be ready to help heal others when the need arises. *The Messiah, the story tells us, is sitting among the poor, binding his wounds one at a time, waiting for the moment when he will be needed. So it is, too, with the minister. Since it is his task to make visible the first vestiges of liberation for others, he must bind his own wounds carefully in anticipation of the moment when he will be needed.*

We all have bruises and ailments, and some of them will never be completely healed in this life. Even so, God's grace is available and sufficient to grant us what we need to care for our own needs and still help others. In 2 Corinthians 12:7-10, the apostle Paul petitions the Lord to remove a personal impediment, but God chooses not to do so and notes that the impediment has a significant and necessary purpose, *for my power is made perfect in weakness.*

The miracle of perfecting and projecting healing and strength is tied to our commitment and efforts to lift others despite our own pain and impediments. *I delight in weaknesses, in insults, in hardships, in persecutions, in difficulties. For when I am weak, then I am strong*, was the apostle Paul's mindset in response to Christ choosing not to remove the personal impediments that Paul had asked the Lord to remove.

So I have learned to dress my wounds daily in God's grace and reach out to help others, thereby making my own weaknesses a vehicle of healing and inspiration for others. Daily we must treat our outer and inner wounds, so we can be ready immediately to help others. Outer wounds refer to those that are exposed and may be seen or touched. They may require bandages, braces, ointments, and other treatments. We must speedily and appropriately dress outer wounds so we can start the healing process or at least not contribute to further hurt. *Inner wounds* are our covered hurts, which may require internal treatments and mental care. In addition to appropriate medications and procedures, our environment and daily diet greatly affect our inner wellness.

My daily practice, as an injured warrior, is to bandage my own wounds by returning to my beginnings to seek a greater understanding of the "what, why, and how" of my lived and inborn hurts. The better I understand the truth of the "what, why, and how" of my wounds, the more effectively I can treat them and help those among whom I live and work.

Nowhere else have I found a more effective model for healing and lifting others than the story demonstrated in the pages of the Bible, which provides a historical and inspirational record of God, his people (Israel), and his plan for the redemption of mankind. The Bible provides abundant evidence that the power of knowing one's story can heal and guide an individual and a nation triumphantly through the darkest of days, perpetually. While everyone has a personal historical journey, the great common phenomenon is that we all have a history and heritage that genealogically leads back to wholeness and unity with the same Creator. How awesome and inspiring is that! So wholeness is the ultimate beauty and assurance that comes from knowing the "what, why, and how" of our brokenness and provides us the healing and guidance for living triumphantly and lifting others in the communities where we live and work.

Helping to heal and lift others requires us to continually anoint and dress our own wounds by connecting with the genealogical and psychological lessons from our past. Interestingly, our history and heritage hold invaluable keys to our current personal struggles. The wellness journey begins for each of us when we embrace self-awareness and self-identity. Too often we seek passionately to lift others but lack the strength and endurance because we ourselves are ailing and need both treatment and strength for the heavy lift. Often, we see seemingly good-hearted people and organizations providing handouts (goods) and benefits to the needy rather than helping them to stand on their own, lifting their communities, and inspiring generational success among their posterity.

Procreant servant leadership is about the process of creating leaders for our communities who not only help others, but help them to help themselves and inspire a spirit of generative servant leadership in the communities where they live and work. This journey requires one to **embrace** self-awareness and self-identity, **develop** biblically based character, **build** a capacity to serve, and **inspiringly serve** their communities. This style of servant leadership uses the life of Jesus in relationship with his twelve disciples as the principal model for creating procreant servant leaders.

What Is Procreant Servant Leadership and How Is It Different from Other Descriptions of Servant Leadership?

Procreant servant leaders are those who help themselves, help others, help others to help themselves, and inspire a spirit of generative servant leadership among the communities where they live and work. The process for developing procreant servant leaders is called **EDBI** (embracing, developing, building, and inspiring a spirit of generative servant leadership):

- **Embracing** self-awareness and self-identity
- **Developing** biblically based character
- **Building** capacity to serve
- **Inspiring** others to serve

While procreant servant leadership embraces many of the modern teachings about servant leadership, here are some key differences:

- Procreant servant leadership follows a biblically based model for transforming men and women into servant leaders.
- The definition of procreant servant leadership is clearly articulated and can be evaluated.
- Procreant servant leaders inspire a spirit of generative servant leadership in the communities where they live and work.
- The procreant servant leader seeks his own healing (wraps his own wounds) before attempting to transform others and continually seeks wellness and self-improvement.
- The process focuses intently on transforming the lives of selected leaders over time.
- Procreant servant leaders are committed to and driven by the process that Jesus used to transform his twelve disciples.

First, procreant servant leadership provides a biblically based model for developing men and women into servant leaders. The model is intended to closely align with the biblical description of how Jesus transformed his disciples into generative servant leaders, whom he gave the keys to the kingdom of heaven and commissioned to go throughout the world making disciples and creating other servant leaders, perpetually carrying out the work of the ministry of Jesus. Although Robert Greenleaf acknowledged the great works of Jesus and gave him credit as the greatest servant leader of all, in his essay "The Servant as Leader," Greenleaf did not attribute Jesus's relationship with his disciples as the foremost pattern for creating servant leaders.

To the credit of those who have thought deeply and written about the subject of developing servant leaders, many have identified important values and character traits that servant leaders should possess. Further, many authors and speakers point to Jesus and his discipleship ministry as the supreme model for creating servant leaders. Even so, I am not aware of a work or presentation that aligns closely from start to finish, using Jesus's relationship with his disciples as the principal guide for creating servant leaders whose impact is transformative and generative in their communities. This thought is somewhat corroborated by C. Gene Wilkes, who said, "Too many works start with characteristics of a leader and then, if at all, move to Jesus's life and teachings to support those ideas." In short, while many people seem to view servant leadership as a leadership style, few sufficiently provide details about a process for developing effective servant leaders, which leaves a gap between theory and practice. This gap between the theory and practice of servant leadership is what I call the **praxis** of procreant servant leadership.

Secondly, the definition of procreant servant leadership is clearly articulated and can be visualized and evaluated, whereas many definitions of servant leadership are vague and hard to measure. For example, some define a servant leader as one who helps and places the needs of others before their own, thereby increasing morale and inspiring those helped to become happier and more productive. However, when you think about how that looks and how to evaluate the success of the servant leader, it becomes very difficult. I have found that Robert Greenleaf's evaluative questions for determining whether a servant leader is effective are also a great tool for helping to determine what a servant leader is or ought to be. Here are some evaluative questions that Greenleaf proposes for determining the effectiveness of the servant leader:

Do those served grow as persons? Do they, while being served, become healthier, wiser, freer, more autonomous, more likely themselves to become servants? And what is the effect on the least privileged in society? Will they benefit or at least not be further deprived?

Jesus's life in relation to the development of his twelve disciples is the primary tool for defining procreant servant leadership; however, when comparing Greenleaf's evaluative questions, they seem to align with what a procreant servant leader is expected to be.

Procreant servant leaders are those who do the following:

- Help themselves (wrap their own wounds) **(not evaluated by Greenleaf)**
- Help others, help others to help themselves. **(grow as persons, becoming healthier, wiser, freer, more autonomous)**
- Inspire a spirit of generative servant leadership among the communities where they live and work **(more likely themselves to become servants)**

- Consider the effect on the least privileged in society **(whether they will benefit or at least not be further deprived)**

Thirdly, procreant servant leadership has a generative focus. The idea is that those who are transformed help to inspire a spirit of servant leadership in their communities that reproduces perpetually. The process leads to a culture of continual self-help and self-sustainment community-wide, where all instinctively work together for a healthy, Godfearing environment. This is in contrast to many of the modern descriptions of servant leadership, which seem to view servant leadership as a quick fix for improving productivity in businesses and organizations. Here is a blurb from an article that seeks to promote servant leadership as a win-win style of leadership for businesses:

Servant leaders believe that when their team members feel personally and professionally fulfilled, they produce higher-quality work more efficiently and productively. . . . [This] is important in business because it creates a work environment in which employees at all levels of your organization feel respected, appreciated, and valued.

Even though this view of the expected outcomes of servant leadership may be true in some respects, employee happiness, customer satisfaction, and company profits alone present a narrow view of the expected outcomes of effective servant leadership as defined by Greenleaf and exemplified in the life of Jesus in relation to his twelve disciples.

In contrast to the quote above, it should be noted that the focus of Jesus's servant leadership program was not on meeting all of the physical and emotional needs of the multitudes of his day. His main ministry among his disciples was to create servant leaders who would help to transform people, who would subsequently lead a transforming institution, the church, that would change their communities and society perpetually.

Fourthly, the procreant servant leader seeks his own healing (wraps his own wounds) before attempting to transform others and continually seeks wellness and self-improvement. In this context, self-help may be described as individuals having the social, emotional, mental, and physical capabilities to help themselves. They are self-aware, have high self-esteem, are sufficiently skilled in a ministry area, and effectively use their skills and abilities to help themselves and those for whom they have responsibility. The servant leader is not perfect, but to ensure that her own injuries do not become an impediment to helping others, she wraps them diligently.

It may be suggested that Jesus spent his early years in self-development, which may help to explain why the Scriptures share little about his life as a child. Luke 2:52 says that Jesus grew and ". . . increased in wisdom and stature, and in favour with God and man." Later in Jesus's life, Luke (3:23) tells us, "Jesus himself was about thirty years old when he began his ministry."

At any rate, procreant servant leaders are those who not only have the capacity to help, but also have experienced a level of wellness and success in their own lives that allows them to help others heal and achieve for themselves, so that those helped may in turn help others and inspire in others a spirit of generative servant leadership.

Take, for example, the Good Samaritan. In this highly illustrative story, Jesus shared with his disciples an example of what a neighborly person may look like. Also, he provides us with an example of the actions and qualities of a great servant leader. The protagonist in the parable is a Samaritan, a non-Jew, who in New Testament times was considered by Jewish people to be less than themselves and unclean. Yet it is the Samaritan who saves and serves a distressed Jew, thereby demonstrating that the Samaritan possesses a high level of self-awareness and self-identity, biblically based character, capacity to help himself and others, and power to liberate and commission his oppressor to serve in a similar capacity.

In the parable, the Samaritan followed a path that had been recently traveled by two Jewish men of great distinction. Along the path, he found a Jew who had been robbed, beaten, and left for dead along the road. Unlike the two distinctive servant leaders who traveled ahead of him, the Samaritan stopped, provided aid to the hurting man, placed the victim on his beast, and presumably walked, perhaps guiding the animal as it carried the injured man to safety. After finding a safe location where the injured could gain medical treatment, the Samaritan paid for his healthcare and entered into an agreement with the healthcare provider to cover the cost of future treatment to allow the injured traveler to regain his health. This story was told by Jesus as an illustration of a neighborly person. However, rarely do I hear ministers and teachers speaking about the social, emotional, and physical well-being of the good Samaritan. What can we deduce from a story like this about the good Samaritan as a servant leader?

One thing we can suggest is that the man had an appreciation for humanity, the sanctity of life. Without knowing the individual or caring about the injured person's sex, race, or religion, the traveler was moved by the apparent fact that another human being had been injured and was in need. His passion pushed past his concern for his own personal well-being to the point where he chose to risk his own safety, health, and wealth to assist someone who had a need greater than his own. Despite the social norms and customs of the day, despite the fact that other Jewish religious leaders chose to pass the injured man without aiding him, despite the danger that he would put himself in by stopping to help the injured man, and despite the likelihood that his own purpose for traveling the Jericho Road would be greatly delayed or forfeited, the Samaritan willingly stopped to help. So regardless of the myriad of good reasons he may have had not to stop, this man had the social, emotional, mental, physical, and economic wellness and courage to stop to help the injured man. This may suggest to us that this man was well or secure enough in his communal thinking to realize that any human being in need is worth helping.

Another thing it may suggest to us is that this man's heart to help was greater than his fear of failure. His passion to help the injured man was stronger than his urge not to get involved. As Martin Luther King Jr. said in his "I've Been to the Mountaintop" speech, *perhaps the Good Samaritan thought less about what would happen to him if he stopped to help the injured man and thought more about what would happen to the man if he did not stop and help him.* The idea that the good Samaritan felt compelled by a sense of duty to stop and help the injured man speaks volumes about the social and emotional stability of the Good Samaritan. He exemplified a willingness to lay down his life for the life of his brother.

Lastly, we can presume that the Good Samaritan was in good shape physically and well off financially. He was able to help the injured onto his (the Samaritan's) beast and probably walked a relatively great distance to take the injured man to get help. He not only took the man to get assistance, but he also paid for the injured man's care and agreed to cover the cost of future care needed to nurse the injured man back to health. Perhaps the most important thing that the good Samaritan gave that day was his time. Being a person of good health and sufficient wealth, and perhaps a notable business person, he, like the priest and Levite, may have been justified in the eyes of others in bypassing the injured man for the sake of his own safety and well-being. In lieu of placing himself in danger and derailing his business for the day, society may have thought it admirable for the Good Samaritan to have just sped into town, alerted the authorities, and perhaps paid to have someone come back and help the injured man. In this way, he could have been safe himself and a doer of good deeds.

The main point to be made in this reflection is that the good Samaritan had sufficiently wrapped his own wounds and was prepared to minister to the injured Jew without allowing his social, emotional, mental, or physical impediments to prevent his efforts to minister to the needy.

Fifthly, procreant servant leadership focuses intently on transforming the lives of selected leaders over time.

When Jesus was ready to begin his ministry, he selected twelve ordinary men, who would take up and carry out the work that he established for them. The twelve witnessed and experienced firsthand Jesus's love and work of salvation for people. He worked with them for about three years, actively sharing his love for them and teaching them to do the same for others. At the end of a three-year discipleship, Jesus commissioned his students as servant leaders and charged them to take on the responsibility to actively share His love and salvation with all people, from generation to generation, worldwide. He empowered them with knowledge and the promise of His enduring presence. Then he left the work to them.

This description presumes that a servant leader is not merely one who goes around doing good deeds—not to minimize the need for doing good deeds, but doing good deeds does not make one a servant leader. Truthfully, all Christians are required by Jesus to do good to others; this is a tenet of the Christian faith. But being kind and generous is far from what it means to be a servant leader. In reality, you do not have to be a Christian to do good deeds. Anybody can be generous and do good deeds for others. For example, a grocery assistant (bag boy) may earn a lot of praise from onlookers for helping people pack and load groceries in their cars throughout the week, but over the weekend, that same helpful young man may be a part of a theft ring, taking from the same people he previously helped.

A servant leader is a helper,
But not every helper is a servant leader.

Sixth and finally, procreant servant leaders are committed to and driven by the process, which commissions them to become transformative and generative leaders in their communities.

Even though Jesus gave his disciples the great commission and empowered them with knowledge and the promise of his enduring presence, it was not until ten days after Jesus's ascension that the disciples received the power to begin their transformative and generative outreach mission. This was all a part of the process, and Jesus required that his disciples follow it.

Jesus's servant leader development program was so effective that it grew from a small group with eleven servant leaders at Jesus's death into the world's largest religion in the twenty-first century, practiced by nearly a third (31 percent) of Earth's 7.3 billion people, according to a Pew Research report by Hackett and McClendon.

Remarkably, Jesus only spent about three years training his disciples. Even more remarkable is that he called and used people with ordinary skills and resources who were not religious leaders. And perhaps most remarkable is that the fellowship of believers, the church, did not begin active membership intake until after the death of Jesus. So the church's great evangelistic movement was not launched while Jesus was on earth. He was not physically present on the day of Pentecost, and consequently, the initial leadership for the local church's expansion was left in the hands of a small number of servant leaders.

Chapter 1
The *Praxis* of Procreant Servant Leadership

What is a procreant servant leader and how is one created? What must a person learn and what skills must he or she master to become an effective procreant servant leader? What process must one follow to move from being a "servant" to becoming a "servant leader"? How is the servant leader's progress measured? Who are the instructors, and what qualifications or skills must they possess? Answers to these questions will help us fill the gap between theory and practice, which is what I call the praxis of procreant servant leadership, the purpose of this book. Praxis may be defined as the "process by which a theory, lesson, or skill is enacted, embodied, or realized. Praxis may also refer to the act of engaging, applying, exercising, realizing, or practicing ideas."

In an effort to better understand servant leadership, I seem to have stumbled onto a gap in the literature for providing clear answers to many of the above questions, especially as it relates to articulating and implementing an effective process that individuals and institutions can follow to create effective procreant servant leaders for communities. My challenge began with finding a good definition for what a servant leader is. Most of the definitions I found seemed to define a servant leader as one who serves others first and cares for the needs of others above him or herself—such a definition is filled with many questions and is definitely very hard to measure. Even more elusive was my search for a program, plan, or process for producing servant leaders for society. Many of the processes referenced the lives of leaders such as Jesus, Gandhi, Martin Luther King Jr., Mother Teresa, etc. and discussed a list of values that characterized the lives of these people, but very few provided details of a process for creating a servant leader.

This book attempts to clearly define the term *servant leader* and provide a framework for creating procreant servant leaders for our communities. Let's begin by examining a couple of popular "modern" definitions for *servant leadership* and then consider the definition for *procreant servant leadership*.

Robert Greenleaf, who in 1970 coined the term *servant-leader*, said, "The servant-leader is servant first . . . *It begins with the natural feeling that one wants to serve, to* *serve first. Then conscious choice brings one to aspire to lead. That person is sharply different from one who is leader first, perhaps because of the need to assuage an unusual power drive or to acquire material possessions . . . The leader-first and the servant-first are two extreme types. Between them, there are shadings and blends that are part of the infinite variety of human nature.*

In addition to his definition, Greenleaf provides a set of guiding questions to test the effectiveness of the servant leader in creating other servant leaders. *The difference manifests itself in the care taken by the servant-first to make sure that other people's highest-priority needs are being served. The best test, and difficult to administer, is: Do those served grow as persons? Do they, while being served, become healthier, wiser, freer, more autonomous, more likely themselves to become servants? And, what is the effect on the least privileged in society? Will they benefit or at least not be further deprived?*

An article by the National Society of Leadership and Success says, *Servant leadership is a style based on the desire to serve and give to your community. By putting the needs of others first, you empower people to perform at their best. When members of the community see your passion and your commitment through your actions, they want to be connected to you.*

The article goes on to say, Anyone can be a leader. Everyone has leadership skills within them, they're all just at differing developmental stages. It takes time to practice and strengthen them; you must invest in developing those skills and committing to growth. Becoming a servant-leader means putting the needs of others before your own and continuously developing . . .

Both Greenleaf and the National Society of Leadership and Success provide definitions for servant leadership and speak highly about the positive effects servant leaders may have on society and within organizations. Unfortunately, neither lays out a process or parameters for moving from *servant* to *servant leader*. So the individual or institution that wants to become or develop servants into servant leaders is left to grapple with unpacking the definition and devising a process that trains, transforms, commissions, and measures the effectiveness of the servant leader. Some questions include: What is meant by becoming a servant first? What qualifies as acceptable service, and who determines when one has served long enough to move from a servant to a servant leader? Once an individual makes a conscious choice to aspire to become a servant leader, what's next? Is there a transformational process, and if so, what does it entail? Is there a model to follow that has been tested?

To the credit of those who have thought deeply and written about the subject of developing servant leaders, many have identified important steps and characteristic traits that may greatly benefit individuals, groups, churches, businesses, and institutions who are seeking to become and/or create servant leaders. Interestingly, many authors and speakers point to Jesus and his discipleship ministry as the supreme model for creating servant leaders. However, lacking in many writings and presentations is a strategy that aligns closely from start to finish, using Jesus's relationship with his disciples as a guide for creating servant leaders whose impact is transformative and generative in their communities. C. Gene Wilkes said it nicely, "Too many works start with characteristics of a leader and then if at all, move to Jesus's life and teachings to support those ideas." In short, while many writers on the subject seem to view servant leadership as a leadership style, few sufficiently provide details regarding a process for developing effective servant leaders. This leaves a gap between theory and practice, the praxis or gap.

The praxis of procreant servant leadership offers an expanded definition of servant leadership, called *procreant servant leadership*, and presents a strategy that closely aligns with key guiding aspects of Jesus's discipleship ministry with his twelve disciples. Although the strategy acknowledges some of Robert Greenleaf's ideas about servant leadership, more importantly, it uses the life of Jesus and his relationship with his apostles as the supreme model for developing, implementing, and assessing a servant leadership program that is transformative and inspires a generative spirit of servant leadership in individuals and communities throughout the world.

Here are some questions that may help to guide our reflective analysis:

- What is servant leadership? Are servants and servant leaders synonymous?

- Are there distinctive qualities and skills that an effective servant leader must possess?
- How does one acquire or improve those skills and qualities?
- Who creates, trains, or leads the servant-leader transformation process?
- What does the process look like, or what are the parameters that guide the aspiring servant leader?
- How do we know when the servant leader is ready to lead?
- How does one measure the success of the servant leader?

These questions and more are addressed in this book.

Chapter 2
A Deeper Dive into the *Leadership* of Procreant Servant Leadership

In several ways, as briefly discussed upfront, procreant servant leadership differs from or perhaps expands the modern descriptions of servant leadership, starting with its definition.

Many modern definitions of servant leadership are rather vague and seem to suggest that the servant leader is simply a servant who gains his influence by always putting the needs of others first. He is a helper at heart, who embraces giving more than receiving. So the more he serves others and put their needs above his own, the greater influence he will have on those served and on humanity in general. And while procreant servant leadership embraces this view, it offers a definition of servant leadership that is more distinctive and measurable, focusing on the role the servant leader plays in lifting others and inspiring them to lift one another generatively. In essence, servant leadership is about helping people to build strong, self-sustaining communities where everyone plays a role in advancing the well-being of themselves and society. Also, the definition of procreant servant leadership helps individuals and institutions create programs that produce servant leaders who are ready to lead in the areas for which they have been prepared.

Often when I read articles or listen to presentations about servant leadership, most of the emphasis is on helping others, especially the poor and disabled. Articles and presentations are replete with great examples of Jesus and other servant leaders who loved humanity and gave sacrificially to lift the hurting and helpless. Without a doubt, scripture makes it abundantly clear that serving others is the job of every believer and that individuals who do so will be handsomely rewarded, especially in eternity. So it is certain from Scripture that Christian service is the hallmark of Christianity.

However, it is very important to understand that being a servant is not the same as being a servant leader, nor does being an excellent servant qualify one to become a servant leader. A leader inspires and helps move people in a direction or achieve a goal. Procreant servant leaders are those who help others help themselves and inspire a spirit of generative servant leadership among the communities in which they live and work.

The role of a procreant servant leader is to inspire individuals and communities to help one another and create servant leaders for their communities. This definition of what a servant leader is and what he or she does enables individuals and institutions to visualize and institute a systematic process to help people lift themselves, build capacity in themselves and their communities, and inspire a spirit of community self-help that is perpetual.

Servants and Servant Leaders
Reflect with me for a few minutes on the meaning of *servant* and *servant leader*, after which I will draw some comparisons or distinctions between the two and offer an expanded definition for servant leadership, one that I call *procreant servant leadership*.

Servant: A servant is one who helps others by providing goods, services, and support or providing acts of kindness, love, and mercy. In the Old and New Testaments, there were various types of servants, such as bond servants or slaves, indentured servants, voluntary indentured servants, and voluntary servants: public servants, social servants, Christian servants, etc.

For some, the word *servant* has a negative connotation, as it is connected to slavery or some form of indentured servitude, where people are forced to work for others against their will. And in many cultures throughout history, this terrible form of servitude has been the case. However, in the New Testament, Jesus brought to light a different type of servitude: one where service was sovereign, one where the most powerful or greatest in the sight of Christendom voluntarily provided goods and services or performed good deeds or kind acts for others. Jesus expressly taught his disciples that this new way of thinking about greatness was in stark contrast to how secular leaders and high governing officials exercise control over others and view greatness. Additionally, he impressed upon his disciples that they were to serve humanity and one another.

Serving humanity: Voluntary service to humanity was a great part of Jesus's earthly ministry. Early in his ministry, Jesus announced that "The Spirit of the Lord is on me because he has anointed me to proclaim good news to the poor. He has sent me to proclaim freedom for the prisoners and recovery of sight for the blind, to set the oppressed free." Although Jesus was rejected in his hometown of Nazareth, he was accepted by many others as he went about ministering. "Jesus went throughout Galilee, teaching in their synagogues, proclaiming the good news of the kingdom, and healing every disease and sickness among the people. News about him spread all over Syria, and people brought to him all who were ill with various diseases, those suffering severe pain, the demon-possessed, those having seizures, and the paralyzed; and he healed them. Large crowds from Galilee, the Decapolis, Jerusalem, Judea and the region across the Jordan followed him" (Matt. 4:23-25).

A great example of Christian service to humanity is found in Luke 10:25-37, where Jesus teaches about the responsibility of believers to be kind and neighborly to all, especially those in need. This parable helped the learners understand the responsibility they have to treat all humanity with kindness and mercifully help others who are in need regardless of race or nationality. It especially underscores the notion that believers are expected to be neighborly both as a duty and as an example to others.

Serving one another: Although Jesus spent a great deal of his life serving humanity, he frequently pulled away from the crowds to spend focused time with his disciples, teaching and ministering to them. He not only served them, but he taught them to love and serve one another. On several occasions, Jesus made it clear among his disciples that they were to strengthen and serve one another. Once, when some of his disciples were upset and discussing among themselves who was the greatest, Jesus took the opportunity to explain to them a new idea for greatness among them. He said to them, *You know that the rulers of the Gentiles lord it over them, and their high officials exercise authority over them. Not so with you. Instead, whoever wants to become great among you must be your servant, and whoever wants to be first must be your slave* (Matt. 20:26-28). He continued by telling them that he was actually their servant, and in numerous ways he demonstrated that he was physically committed to this new leadership concept he presented to them. Jesus said to them that he did not come for them to serve him, but he came to serve them and give his life for them. In serving his disciples, Jesus demonstrated to them how to serve others and commanded them to do the same for one another. Near the time when he would be betrayed unto his death, Jesus had a final meal with his disciples. After the meal, *he got up from the meal, took off his outer clothing, and wrapped a towel around his waist. After that, he poured water into a basin and began to wash his disciples' feet, drying them with the towel that was wrapped around him. . . . I have set you an example that you should do as I have done for you. Very truly I tell you, no servant is greater than his master* (John 13:1-17). Jesus made it clear to his disciples that serving one another was a directive, not an option. Christian servants are those who willingly submit themselves to be governed by biblical teachings as it relates to helping and performing acts of kindness to humanity and one another.

The leader must be the chief servant.
So all Christians are servants to humanity and to one another, and in this way, all can be important because all can serve. However, while Jesus served and ministered to all, he did not call all to be one of his apostles, nor did he give all believers the keys of responsibility for leading the newly established church in Acts 2. Rather, he individually called, mentored, empowered, and commissioned his apostles to serve as foundational leaders in the early

church. He prepared and sent them forth as servant leaders.

The servant leader: In the model that Jesus gave us, he loved and served all people indiscriminately, and he commanded all believers to serve others and one another. However, he only selected twelve men he would dedicate himself to mentoring and preparing to serve as foundational leaders for the early church. Jesus's apostles performed the tasks of training and developing other believers and commissioning them to take up the work to build and edify the body of Christ. Not only did they minister to other believers, but they were helpers and guides to all of humanity in the various communities where they served. These servants were leaders, those who helped and influenced others to respond by following the example and call to service. Servant leaders are not just helpers of humanity, but they are deliberate in their efforts to build capacity in others and to inspire them to become servant leaders who will help themselves, help others, and inspire a spirit of generative servant leadership in their communities.

Characteristics of a servant leader: Aside from serving others, here are a few distinguishing qualities of a procreant servant leader:

- **Selective mentoring** – Jesus served multitudes, but he only mentored twelve. Perhaps it is because mentoring is a connective process that is time-consuming and can only be done effectively in small numbers, so God only gave him twelve. Prior to selecting his disciples, Jesus prayed to God the father all night. He committed himself to them and lost only Judas, because he was the son of perdition.
- **Wellness focus** – The mentor is committed to ministering wellness to his mentees. He helps them embrace their innateness and connectedness to their roots for healing and wholeness. True healing requires connection to the source, which flows from the roots that connect to the source. The miracle is that every human's genealogy eventually connects back to the creator.
- **Capacity building** – The mentor helps mentees to identify their gifts and talents and expand so they will be able to help others to help themselves and their communities.

- **Generative inspiration** – The mentor inspires a spirit of generative servant leadership in his or her mentees. The purpose for the mentoring process is to eventually commission and empower mentees to become servant leaders who inspire and lift others to do the same, perpetually.

In the New Testament, there were several types of servant leaders. Some servant leaders were appointed, some were elected, and some assumed their positions as they filled unmet needs in the church community. In this section, I will briefly share some views regarding each of these categories of servant leaders.

Appointed servant leaders: These are servant leaders who have been called and given authority or commissioned to serve by a governing official or body. For example, in the early church, the Holy Spirit called Paul and Barnabas to servitude, moved on the hearts of men to accept them, anointed them, and sent them off for the work that God had called them to do. In a doctrinal sense, Jesus calls and positions leadership for local churches to serve and care for the members. These called-out ministers are more than servants; they are leaders. This is expressly shared in Ephesians 4:11-15:

> *So Christ himself gave the apostles, the prophets, the evangelists, the pastors and teachers, to equip his people for works of service, so that the body of Christ may be built up until we all reach unity in the faith and in the knowledge of the Son of God and become mature, attaining to the whole measure of the fullness of Christ. Then we will no longer be infants, tossed back and forth by the waves, and blown here and there by every wind of teaching and by the cunning and craftiness of people in their deceitful scheming. Instead, speaking the truth in love, we will grow to become in every respect the mature body of him who is the head, that is, Christ.*

In the above passage, the positions and titles are designated, and the expected outcome is clear. These servant leaders work cooperatively in the local church to ensure that the members grow and develop in unity as they advance in their relationship with Christ and one another. The goal is to create congregations that are strong and capable of acting independently, yet working collaboratively to carry out the mission of the Church Universal while serving as a beacon light of hope for the world, who will see it as a city on a hill that cannot be hidden or ignored.

The example above does not mean that appointed servant leaders may only come from the category of titles listed in Ephesians 4:11. However, it is an example of leaders who are appointed to serve as leaders in the local church. I think that servant leaders may also be appointed in other ways and among other organizations. Another way that a servant leader may obtain a position is via election.

Elected-appointed servant leaders: These are servant leaders chosen by vote or some other method of selection by church congregants, caucuses, conclaves, community members, legislative bodies, etc. Examples of elected servant leaders may include deacons, worship leaders, outreach leaders, public service leaders, community organizers, etc. A biblical example of people selecting their servant leaders is in Acts 6:1-10.

Until this time, it appears that Jesus's apostles were still functioning as the primary servant leaders for overseeing the administration of resources to the widows, as recorded in Acts 6:1-10. This passage of Scripture says that there arose murmuring and disputing among the Hebrew and Grecian believers because the needs of some widows were not being adequately served, while others were receiving the care they needed. The problems seemed to be along racial and cultural lines. This issue came to the attention of the apostles, who seemed to have been continuing to carry out the responsibility for overseeing the administration of funds and resources for the needy.

In prior chapters, there were accounts of some believers selling property and bringing the proceeds to the disciples, who ensured that the needs of the poor were being met. However, to properly handle this issue, the apostles decided to anoint and commission more servant leaders who would ensure that the needs of those widows were properly met and that a system was in place to deal with similar issues that might arise. Additionally, it would free the apostles to focus more reverently on ministering the word of God. This, too, was a rendering of great service to God and his people. So the apostles instructed the community of believers to look among themselves for men who were suitable for the work—men who were full of the

Holy Spirit and wisdom, who had demonstrated maturity in the faith and actively applied the knowledge of the word of God to their own lives. The believers were to pick (elect/select) men whom they had observed to be faithful and able to carry out this great task of ministering to the needs of the poor and less fortunate. Once the men had been chosen (elected/selected), the apostles prayed over them, laid their hands on them, and appointed them to take over the work of ministering to the needs of the people by ensuring that resources were distributed appropriately. These newly appointed servant leaders were very effective in carrying out their responsibilities because the Scriptures said, *So the word of God spread. The number of disciples in Jerusalem increased rapidly, and a large number of priests became obedient to the faith* (Acts 6:7).

This is a great example of the need for servant leaders in our congregations and communities to help meet the needs of the poor and resolve issues that inhibit the growth and well-being of the church and the community. In addition to appointed and elected servant leaders, some servant leaders just seem to assume servant-leader duties.

Self-assumed servant leaders: These are leaders who walk into or work into servant leadership positions by serving and leading others as opportunities present themselves. They are not humanly appointed, nor elected. They gain their influence by voluntarily helping others and meeting critical community needs that otherwise may go unmet. They seek neither position nor recognition; they are the Good Samaritans of the communities where they live and work. Members of local neighborhoods and communities are often keenly aware of who these people are and often look to them for non-politically motivated community leadership. Even appointed and elected servant leaders may seek to gain the insight and influence of self-assumed servant leaders in supporting their work or events. Examples of assumed servant leaders may be food pantry organizers, parent or booster club coordinators, community watch group leaders, boys and girls mentoring group leaders, and various other community and group leaders who serve people and influence others to help themselves and their communities. They are often humble but passionate about what they do and usually volunteer their services.

Although Jesus was anointed and appointed to his work by God his father, in his human form or in terms of earthly government, the Scriptures do not indicate that he was called or appointed by any religious, political, or community group to be their leader. At the time of his choosing and God's leading, Jesus announced his call to ministry and began to serve others without the need for a position assignment, confirmation, or recognition by others. In this sense, Jesus was a self-assumed servant leader.

As a self-assumed servant leader, Jesus announced his debut to serve humanity when he read from Isaiah's prophecy as recorded in Luke 4:18-19 *to proclaim good news to the poor. He has sent me to proclaim freedom for the prisoners and recovery of sight for the blind, to set the oppressed free, to proclaim the year of the Lord's favor.* He did not seek political or financial support from governing bodies, community groups, religious organizations, or philanthropists. He came preaching and teaching without any publicly recognized credentials or supporting groups. Jesus's self-assumed model of servant leadership shows the simplicity and sophistication involved in becoming this type of servant leader. It is simple in that anyone at any level can become a servant leader regardless of heritage and culture, economic status, academic credentials, or social status. Jesus's life perfectly illustrates the simplicity of becoming a self-assumed servant leader.

Jesus's heritage and culture, as was true for many others of his day and time, were that of a normal Jewish boy from Nazareth, although he was in the lineage of David and Abraham. His father and mother kept the standard Jewish festivals, and their place was as common citizens among others of their time. In fact, when Jesus returned to announce his calling, the people of Nazareth recognized him as the son of Joseph and Mary—that is to say, no one of distinction or notoriety.

Economically, Jesus grew up among average working people who needed to earn their living by employing a trade. It is said that Jesus was a carpenter by trade and that he grew up with his brothers and sisters in Nazareth. Though he was wise beyond his years, academically astute, and very well versed in the scripture as evident in his conversations with doctors of the law and the Jewish religious leaders, he was also adept at understanding and speaking plainly to ordinary men and women, using parables to ensure they understood and remembered his teachings.

Socially, outside of mentoring his disciplines and visiting the synagogue, Jesus did not appear to be a part of a social or religious group such as the Elders, Essenes, Pharisees, Priests, Sadducees, Sanhedrin, Scribes, or Zealots. This does not mean that Jesus was antisocial. Jesus spent much of his time interacting with people as he taught and ministered to individuals of various ethnic and social groups. Jesus also visited and dined with a variety of people. What we see in Jesus's ministry is that belonging to a social group is not required to become an effective servant leader. In some ways, depending on the group's legacy and the expectations and views of its members, serving others may be hindered.

Position or title: One of the most significant things about the self-assumed leader is that he or she does not need a position or title to authorize, legitimize, or validate his leadership. This is the new norm that Jesus introduced among his disciples while they argued over who was the greatest among them. Jesus said that the greatest person was the greatest servant. Thinking of greatness in this way suggests that everyone can be great because everyone can serve. So a servant leader does not need to wait until he is appointed or elected to a position to serve, but a servant leader can help others whenever he recognizes a need that he can meet and help others to learn to help themselves, help others, and inspire a spirit of generative servant leadership among the community.

On the other hand, Jesus's life demonstrates the complexity involved in becoming an effective servant leader. Remember, a servant leader is much more than living a life dedicated to helping others—that's the servant part. The leadership part is that of teaching others to help themselves, teaching them to help others, and inspiring a spirit of generative servant leadership in the communities you serve. Becoming a servant leader requires one to embrace self-awareness and self-identity, develop biblically based character, demonstrate love for themselves and others, build capacity in others to serve, and inspire others to serve their communities. Developing servants into servant leaders is a challenging process that takes time. The life of Jesus and his relationship with his twelve apostles gives us a glimpse of the most successful model ever used for developing, implementing, and assessing a servant leadership program that is transformative and inspires a generative spirit of servant leadership in local communities and throughout the world. The elements of the process will be discussed in the next chapter.

In addition to the developmental process, servant leaders will find that there are multitudes of legitimate needs that are pressing and vying for attention. The burden of deciding which needs to be met and which to delay can be overwhelming. The key is to know to whom or what God has called you and circle and fence your time of service. People experience so much brokenness and have so many needs that a servant leader can spend a lifetime serving humanity and die with seemingly little to show in terms of community progression or self-sustainment. Jesus seemed to understand this perfectly regarding his ministry and modeled for us how to balance serving the needy while building capacity and inspiring in others a spirit of generative servant leadership.

First of all, Jesus knew that with each day and each generation, there would arise new and varying needs among humanity. Jesus helps his disciples understand this in Mark 14:3-9. In this passage, a woman came to Jesus while he was reclining at dinner and anointed his head with some very expensive perfume that was worth about a year's wages for a working person of that time. When the disciples saw this, they were very upset and viewed it as a waste of valuable resources that could have been spent meeting the needs of the poor. Not only did the disciples express their disapproval to one another, but they harshly rebuked the woman. Then Jesus said to them *Leave her alone. . . . Why are you bothering her? She has done a beautiful thing to me. The poor you will always have with you, and you can help them any time you want. But you will not always have me. She did what she could. She poured perfume on my body beforehand to prepare for my burial* (Mark 14:3-9). Now, for many people, this may seem to be a selfish, insensitive, and coldhearted statement. And I am sure if it was not Jesus himself who said these words, many Christians today would join the disciples in decrying the waste of this valuable resource when many poor people could have benefited from these wasted resources.

But let's look a little closer to see what we can learn from Jesus's response. Upfront we notice that Jesus is unambiguous in his clear directive for those bothering Mary to *Leave her alone. . . . She has done a beautiful thing to me. . . . The poor you will always have with you, and you can help them any time you want.* Did Jesus need perfume on his head? How was it going to help him? Perhaps it was a nice and kind gesture, but was it more important than using this valuable resource to help the needy? Couldn't she have used a little to anoint Jesus and given the rest to help the poor? Does allowing and defending this apparent waste show a human weakness on Jesus's part? Let's look further.

Leave her alone. Essentially, Jesus said to those who were harshly rebuking Mary to stop attempting to correct and chasten her for using the perfume to anoint him. This is a very noteworthy section on which to reflect. What does Jesus teach us about himself in this passage? What does he teach us about humanity? What does he teach us about one another?

Here, Jesus taught that in his humanity, he needed the service of others. The work that the woman was coming to do was needful and acceptable in the eyes of Jesus: *She poured perfume on my body beforehand to prepare for my burial.* This says to us that the human body is temporal and has needs. He also teaches that it is needful for people to serve one another and that believers should be careful and not prevent those whom God has sent to meet the needs of fellow laborers. He taught them to be sensitive to one another and their pressing needs. Some needs are pressing, and we must be sensitive to the working of the Holy Spirit to ensure that we help and do not hinder the good that God is sending others to do. He taught that speaking up to defend what is good and right is the right thing to do. He taught that God uses whomever he chooses to serve him and humanity. He taught that it's okay to use expensive oil in ministry to one another. Jesus not only instructed them to leave her alone, but he affirmed that she was right and spirit led in what she had done.

She has done a beautiful thing. What was so beautiful about what the woman did for Jesus?

- It was beautiful because *she did what she could.* Independent of others, without the consent of the religious leaders or Jesus's disciples, she went into her storehouse and gave to meet a pressing need that had been revealed to her. Although she could not save him from the cross—his body would be physically sacrificed for all of humanity—nor could she go to the cross with Jesus or for him, she could anoint his body with a sweet-smelling offering. She did what she could do

- It was beautiful because she was a woman who was acting in obeyance to the command of God the Father, in honor of his only begotten son. She was a chosen vessel being divinely guided, carrying out a sacred duty that none of us fully appreciate or understand at this point.
- It was beautiful because she ministered to Jesus when no one else seemed to understand that he needed and would be grateful for this open and deeply passionate act of love and sanctity.
- It was beautiful because it represented the sacrificial offering of the woman's time, talents, and resources to someone who was not a member of her inner circle of family and friends. How likely is it that a woman of this day and time would give what may have constituted her life savings or her family's financial security to a non-family member for such a cause? Because this woman blessed Jesus, she did a beautiful thing.

Finally, Jesus explained, *The poor you will always have with you and you can help them any time you want.* Although this seems a little harsh and maybe even selfish, it rings true from generation to generation. The poor have been a part of the world's community since early biblical history. In the Scriptures, the poor are often described as those whose circumstances and situations in life often arose out of no fault of their own. Frequently, the Scriptures list among the poor those who are widows, orphans, displaced, disadvantaged, and disabled, including the blind, lame, deaf, mute, diseased, etc. Sometimes entire regions found themselves among the needy during times of famine or as a result of natural disasters, such as draughts, storms, pestilences, and wars. Even today in America, what do you think might happen to the millions of victims of hurricanes, tornadoes, wildfires, and other disasters that would leave them displaced if it weren't for people helping one another? So the idea that the poor will always be with us is a fact about life on earth.

Jesus knew that he had limited time on earth to proclaim good news to the poor, freedom for the prisoners, and recovery of sight for the blind; to set the oppressed free; and to proclaim the year of the Lord's favor. He knew that as important as these things were, he only had about three years on earth to physically minister to the needs of the people. Also, Jesus knew that he would not eradicate the ills of sickness, disease, and poverty from the earth because it was a condition of life on earth, and from generation to generation, the needy would appear until Jesus returned and created a new heaven and earth. Finally, he also knew that as long as the earth existed, the need would arise for men and women to continue to preach the good news and lead people in the way of righteousness. Therefore, Jesus called and mentored twelve men who would be charged as the initial foundational leaders for the early church as described in Acts 2. These men would continue the same type of ministry that Jesus had begun: they would proclaim the gospel of Christ, call men and women to salvation, establish local congregations, teach and mentor others to spread the word of God, and implement the ministry worldwide. They, too, would heal and minister to the sick and disabled and set the bound and oppressed free. Jesus was committed to transforming his twelve apostles into servant leaders who would help themselves, help others, help others to help themselves, and inspire a spirit of generative servant leadership in their communities and throughout the world. As such, Jesus limited his time with the needy multitudes and spent quality time daily with his disciples to give them the grooming and personal attention they needed to develop as servant leaders.

The Servant and the Servant Leader Tasks Table

Servant	Servant Leader
A servant is one who helps others by providing labor, goods, and services or by performing good deeds or showing acts of kindness, love, and mercy to others.	A servant leader helps others to become leaders who lift themselves and others by serving and inspiring them to become servant leaders in the communities where they live and work. Additionally, the servant leader does the following: Helps (heal) himself and others. Helps others to help themselves. Helps to build capacity in others to serve their communities. Inspires a spirit of generative servant leadership among others.
All Christians are commanded to serve one another and humanity.	Not all Christians are called to be servant leaders.

Christians are called and commanded to be witnesses of Christ, evangelize others and serve one another.	Jesus selected and called his twelve disciples from among many who followed him. He prayed all night before calling his disciples, who were given to him by God. Similarly, the servant leaders in Acts 6 were chosen from among many other believers. They were ready for the work, so the disciples prayed over them and commissioned them into service as servant leaders.
All Christians are members of the body of Christ and have some position of service in the body, but all are not called to positions of leadership.	They may lead in various capacities in local churches, governments, communities, businesses, etc. Servant leaders may acquire their positions in several ways: called or appointed, elected, or assumed.

	Appointed – Religious leaders, civil servants, etc. Elected-appointed – organizational leaders, local church leaders, political officials, etc. Assumed – Community or group advocates, organizer activists, etc.

Chapter 3
The Supreme Model
of Procreant Servant Leadership:
Jesus and His Disciples

In his 1970 essay, "The Servant as Leader," Robert K. Greenleaf presents the significance of servant leadership and discusses the institution as servant, trustee as servant, and teacher as servant. Although the term *servant leadership* was coined and popularized by Robert Greenleaf, truthfully, even by Greenleaf's own admission, servant leadership has been around since biblical days, especially in regard to the life of Jesus, who by far presents the greatest demonstration of the powerful influence that serving others while leading them can have on transforming the lives of those individuals and their communities.

In addition to providing some very thought-provoking ideas about the servant as leader, Greenleaf provides some evaluative questions that help us think deeply about and, in a real sense, measure the success of a servant leader. These questions include, *Do those served grow as persons? Do they, while being served, become healthier, wiser, freer, more autonomous, more likely themselves to become servants?* When leaders shift their mindset and serve first, they benefit along with their employees, as their employees acquire personal growth, while the organization grows due to the employees' growing commitment and engagement.

Unfortunately, when analyzing many definitions of servant leadership, I grapple with clearly understanding what a servant leader is and how to develop such a person. What's the process or model for creating servant leaders? In this chapter, the life and relationship of Jesus with his twelve apostles provides the model for developing procreant servant leaders who help others and inspire a spirit of generative servant leadership in the communities where they live and work.

Institutions desiring to create procreant servant leaders should themselves serve as a premiere model of the leaders and communities they hope to produce. Institutions should project a campus culture and climate where administrators, faculty, and staff actively practice the principles of servant leadership in their relationships among one another and with students. By demonstrating procreant servant leadership, the university cadre provides students an opportunity to live in and observe a community where servant leadership theory is practiced.

Jesus, the Supreme Model: When Jesus was about thirty years old, he felt that the time had come for him to start an important part of his life's work, which was to call and transform twelve ordinary men into servant leaders who would take his finished work of salvation to men and women throughout the world. Up close and personally, the disciples witnessed and experienced the unconditional and indiscriminate love of Jesus for all people worldwide. Jesus worked with his disciples for three years, actively sharing his love for them and teaching them to do the same for others. At the end of a three-year discipleship period with them, Jesus commissioned his students as servant leaders, then empowered and charged them to take on the responsibility of actively sharing God's love and salvation with all people, from generation to generation, worldwide. After empowering them with knowledge and the promise of his enduring presence, he released them to the work of evangelism and church building.

Here are some additional interesting points about Jesus as a servant leader:

- Position is not essential to becoming a great servant leader. Jesus was not selected to serve in a community or political leadership position or capacity. He was not called or ordained by the people to serve as their congregational leader. There was no need for him to seek a position: the needy were plentiful, so he began to serve near his hometown.
- Jesus did not have secular or religious credentials to become a servant leader, although, from the time he was a child, he spent time in temples sitting among teachers, listening to them and asking questions. From a child to about thirty years old, Jesus lived with his family as many other children did, learning and growing in wisdom with man and God, and he was not numbered among the pious Jewish religious leaders.
- Jesus was not a member of a local or national religious or political group. He did not derive power, position, or status from clubs, organizations, or political or religious establishments.

- Jesus sought out and called his mentees from among a variety of ordinary men, who were willing to follow his teachings. He called men who were not qualified as devout and learned religious men.
- The church's great evangelistic movement was not launched while Jesus was on earth. He was not physically present on the day of Pentecost, and subsequently, initial leadership for the church's expansion was left in the hands of a small number of servant leaders, whom he empowered and released for ministry after his death.

For a few minutes, let's look at how Jesus chose his twelve disciples and some of the methods he used to prepare them to become servant leaders.

The "Right Fit" for Jesus's Servant Leader Program: It is clearly documented that Jesus was selective in choosing who would become part of his initial leadership team and his inner circle, the twelve disciples. Although multitudes were drawn to Jesus and sat for hours listening to his teachings and observing his miracles, only twelve were selected to hang out with him as mentees. The twelve are listed by name in Mark 3, Matthew 10, and

Luke 6. Paul's list refers to his inner circle as pillars of the early church in Galatians 2:9.

The following is a summary of the call of Jesus's first disciples:

> *One day as Jesus was standing by the Lake of Gennesaret, the people were crowding around him and listening to the word of God. He saw at the water's edge two boats, left there by the fishermen, who were washing their nets. He got into one of the boats, the one belonging to Simon, and asked him to put out a little from shore. Then he sat down and taught the people from the boat. When he had finished speaking, he said to Simon, Put out into deep water, and let down the nets for a catch. Simon answered, "Master, we've worked hard all night and haven't caught anything. But because you say so, I will let down the nets." When they had done so, they caught such a large number of fish that their nets began to break. So they signaled their partners in the other boat to come and help them, and they came and filled both boats so full that they began to sink. When*

Simon Peter saw this, he fell at Jesus's knees and said, "Go away from me, Lord; I am a sinful man!" For he and all his companions were astonished at the catch of fish they had taken, and so were James and John, the sons of Zebedee, Simon's partners. Then Jesus said to Simon, "Don't be afraid; from now on you will fish for people." So they pulled their boats up on shore, left everything and followed him. Luke 5:1-11.

In this story, we find that Jesus called his first four disciples: Andrew, Simon (Peter), James, and John (sons of Zebedee). Then, like he did in this interesting encounter, he called the other eight of his initial twelve disciples. The manner in which he approached and called them is quite interesting and provides us many great nuggets we can use to apply to evangelism and to finding students who are the "right fit" for creating procreant servant leaders.

It is very important to understand that Jesus deeply loved and sought to help the poor and needy, but helping, healing, and loving everyone is different from choosing everyone to be a ministry leader. While all Christians are called to love and show compassion to the needy, not all Christians are chosen to be servant leaders as the term is defined in this text. Remember, servant leaders are those who help others and inspire a spirit of generative servant leadership among the communities in which they live and work.

In society and among today's Christians, Jesus would probably be described by many as sexist, racist, conceited, and arrogant, among other derogatory expressions, for independently choosing only men that he liked to be a part of his twelve apostles. Even today, people may wonder, Why wasn't his group more diverse? Why weren't some biblical scholars such as priests, elders, scribes, or doctors of the law recruited? Why weren't any women chosen? Why isn't there more kickback to this oppressive leadership style?

To respond in general to some of those questions, it is reasonable to assume that most people of Jesus's day were not interested in Jesus's group because Jesus did not appear to offer any real opportunities for economic advancements or pose any viable threats to the Roman government. The group who seemed to be most visibly threatened by Jesus and his disciples was the Jewish religious leaders, who vowed to kill Jesus, and their plot eventually succeeded.

However, for the general public at large, Jesus and his disciples may have been of little interest, as many other religious leaders had come and gone. So many people may have viewed following Jesus as another fad or cult. Others may have viewed following Jesus as unnecessarily burdensome and risky, for Jesus offered little in terms of physical possessions, but required his followers to be willing to give up everything, including their livelihood and personal pursuits. For these reasons alone, the general public may have taken little interest in Jesus and how he chose his followers. After all, many probably saw the disciples as mere servants who helped Jesus pursue his personal ambitions.

Jesus was sure about his own consciousness and identity as the righteous son of God,
who was equal with God yet esteemed or valued human beings as above his own worth. Perhaps it was this view of the value of people that prompted him to become humble and leave the prominence and power of his

position in righteousness to take on a body of flesh and become a man so that he could satisfy the requirements of the law, to give his life sacrificially.

Chapter 4
Embracing Self-Awareness and Self-Identity Healing Personal Wounds Enables One to Lift and Inspire Others!

From a historical perspective, many well-known and arguably most effective servant leaders have been people who were stable in their personal identity, exemplified strong moral character, demonstrated love and respect for humanity, displayed a commitment to building capacity in others to become servant leaders, and sought to commission others to continue the work of serving humanity perpetually.

A few notable servant leaders included Dr. Martin Luther King Jr., Mahatma Gandhi, and, most notably, Jesus. While all three of these well-known servant leaders were models in many aspects, only Jesus was perfect in his biblically based character. And only Jesus's movement was strategically launched after his death and ascension. It was his followers, impassioned and empowered on the day of Pentecost, who committed themselves to helping others, developing and empowering them to build capacity in others. So today, more than two thousand years later,

Christian servant leaders are fully empowered leaders of homes, congregations, missions, and communities who are excited about serving and leading others in a society of service to humanity and God.

Servant leaders are forerunners in helping and guiding others to become strong, compassionate givers and guardians in neighborly communities. By creating servant leaders, we can ensure that neighborly communities develop and prosper perpetually. Neighborly communities are those that make sure the needs of people around them are met and that a healthy community culture grows and propagates such that society is transformed into a place where people treat others with the same love they show themselves. Servant leaders are practitioners who become adept in loving and responding to the needs of individuals and communities. They are soldiers who fight alongside the warriors they serve. They are mentors, whose lives are portraits for their mentees. The ultimate goal of the servant leader is to help others while teaching them to help themselves, their families, and their communities; serving and leading are reciprocal tenets of servant leadership.

Robert Greenleaf said, *If a better society is to be built, one that is more just and more loving, one that provides greater creative opportunity for its people, then the most open course is to raise both the capacity to serve and the very performance as servant of existing major institutions by new regenerative forces operating within them."*

So, creating servant leaders who live and lead in their communities provides a built-in mechanism of self-help for developing and sustaining productive, healthy, safe, and vibrant communities that embrace high moral values and patrol undesirable behavior. An important question is, what qualities and skills are needed for one to become an effective servant leader? Also, how does one acquire these skills and qualities?

In reflecting on Jesus's life as a servant leader and his preparation of his disciples for servant leadership, it may be noted that Jesus embraced and taught his disciples to embrace self-awareness and self-identity, develop biblically based character, demonstrate love for themselves and others, build capacity in others to serve, and lead by serving and inspiring others to become servant leaders.

Embracing Self-Awareness and Self-Identity: For this discussion, *self-awareness* refers to one having conscious knowledge of his or her own presence or being. It includes consciousness via senses (touch, sight, hearing, smell, taste), desires, actions, and reactions. The term *self-identity* relates to a person's uniqueness or distinctiveness, which includes a person's mental and physical qualities, temperament, and natural and cultural experiences. These innate qualities and cultural experiences cannot be easily changed or altered. Examples of such things include biological parents, gender, genetic makeup, race, birth, and cultural experiences. A person's self-awareness and self-identity work together to help a child form an opinion of who "I" and "me" are. Processing information about oneself and embracing the "I" is very important for helping oneself, which is a prerequisite for lifting others and helping them to help themselves and their communities.

The power of self-awareness in ministry. From the time a mother conceives until the day of birth, a baby is dependent upon the mother for nourishment and protection. During the entire process, the growing fetus has no say so or choice in its source of nourishment, environmental conditions, or ethnic and cultural identity at birth. After birth, babies do not know themselves or their parents, nor do they seem to care. Where they live, what they are wearing, their race, cultural heritage, and socioeconomic status are all inconsequential. So in their early days of life, their cry is generally for comfort and care. It represents their effort to seek the nourishment and comfort needed to survive in a new environment, in which they are unable to help themselves.

Interestingly, while the first few years of a child's life are invaluable in their growth and development, infants are nearly totally dependent on others to teach them who they are and to establish the norms and values that will influence them for life. The environment in which they spend the first two years of their lives will greatly affect their earthly existence for the rest of their lives. This speaks to the enormity of the duty of parenting, especially in the early years of children's lives.

Usually, when a child is about two years old, a seminal moment occurs that changes the child's life forever. The child recognizes his or her image and starts to form an identity. Isn't it amazing that babies recognize the image of their parents and caregivers more than a year before they even recognize their own image?

Before helping others, babies have to get to a point where they can first help themselves. Until they are able to hold their own bottles, they cannot even feed themselves, let alone pour milk into a bottle or mix formula. But as they grow, they develop the strength to do things to help themselves, and learn to identify others and communicate with them, even before they know themselves:

Self-awareness begins to dawn shortly before the second birthday. Numerous studies in developmental psychology have shown that human infants begin to recognize themselves in mirrors and through recording devices (e.g., video) around 18 months of age. When children begin to realize that the images they see in the mirror are themselves, they literally see themselves acting in reflection, and recognize their actions as their own.

In the terms made famous by William James (1892– 1963), the "I" begins to recognize the "Me" as an embodied social actor, as reflected quite literally in such things as mirrors and recording devices, and more figuratively in the mirroring appraisals of others. Once the I is aware of and able to reflect upon itself (the Me), the I can begin to control the presentation of self on the social stage. Assisting in its efforts are powerful social–moral emotions, such as embarrassment, shame, guilt, and pride (Tangney et al., 2007).

Prior to babies being able to recognize themselves, the images they see in mirrors, videos, photos, etc., are impersonal and practically meaningless to them. But a few years later, as the "I" grows, the baby now looks at the photo and compares what he or she sees with what others look like, and often values what he or she sees in relation to what others look like and, more importantly, based on the responses of others to how his pictures and images look.

When the "I" matures to the point where he or she accepts and loves the "me," regardless of the child's physical or mental limitations or what others think or say about him or her, then the child will be able to show high esteem and value for him or herself and others.

One of the great commandments of God is that people should love their neighbors as they love themselves. The implication is that people generally love themselves a lot; therefore, self-love is a great measuring tool for how a person should love others. Alternatively, it may suggest that a person who does not properly love and help himself cannot adequately love and help others.

When I first started to fly on airplanes, I was a little nervous, so I would pray a lot, but also listen very attentively to the instructions from the hostess and captain prior to takeoff. One thing I noticed about every flight is that they all gave similar informational briefs and demonstrations before takeoff. During one part of their presentation, when discussing the use of oxygen masks, the attendant would say that in the case of low pressure, the oxygen mask would automatically drop down from overhead and that each individual should put their own mask on first, before assisting others. Once their mask is on securely, then they may assist others. The point is that passengers can be more effective for longer by first putting on their own mask, helping themselves. In this way, they increase their chance of remaining conscious, and thereby being able to help others who may be in danger. The moral is that we can more effectively help others when we are physically, socially, emotionally, and spiritually self-aware and confident about who we are.

The Scriptures, both Old and New Testaments, share much with the readers to indicate that Jesus was consciously aware of his being, naturally and supernaturally. In Philippians 2, the apostle Paul shares some of the thoughts of the pre-incarnate Christ about his decision to become human. In the passage, Jesus clearly affirms that he is fully aware of where he was and who he was in terms of his righteousness and rightness. Jesus fully understood his relationship with God, the power of his position, and his worth to God and humanity. In fact, I believe that it was his profound awareness of who he was and his valuation of his own self-worth, coupled with his firsthand knowledge of the deep love that God the father had for humanity, that moved him to humbly submit himself as a servant and give his life to save and reconcile humanity to God. This exemplifies the power that self-awareness has to propel a person into purpose and selfless service.

The power of self-identity in ministry. Scripture helps us to understand Jesus's view of his identity from his heavenly position. Jesus realized that he was irrevocably tied to his relationship with God as his only begotten son. He was totally righteous, totally without sin, totally saved, and the heir to riches and righteousness forever. His DNA and heritage made him transcendent to sin. He was equal to God and was above reproach; he *was* God. He understood that his perfection was based on who he was, his identity as the son of God, Philippians 2:1-8.

Jesus understood that he would forever be the loved and cherished son of God, who would never be lost. Although he would be separated from his father for a few brief days as he suffered, bled, and died for the sin of humanity, he could not be lost. On the other hand, if he did not give his life, humanity could not live in a reconciled relationship with God and could never again live as a holy people, in a holy city, in the presence of a holy God (Rev. 21:1-6).

While Jesus realized his oneness with the father in terms of righteousness and preeminence, he understood that the love God had for his lost and imperfect children was just as deep to God as the perfect love he had for his only begotten son. This fact was evident in that God the Father was willing to allow Jesus, the perfect son, to suffer and die to save imperfect humanity. Consequently, the immeasurable love that God had for humanity was personified in the life of Jesus, who loved and valued the salvation of the human race more dearly than he valued saving himself. The Scripture says that Jesus esteemed humanity greater than he did himself. In other words, he valued humanity more than he treasured his own life. This demonstrates the ultimate power of self-identity in ministry.

God was willing to be separated from Jesus to save humanity. Only when we fully recognize who we are, our relationship to God, and the power of our position can we understand the real value of others, love them appropriately, and be humble enough to serve them to the fullest.

It was Jesus's recognition of his own identity in relationship to God's identity that propelled him to calvary. Jesus, *who, being in very nature God, did not consider equality with God something to be used to his own advantage; rather, he made himself nothing by taking the very nature of a servant, being made in human likeness* (Phil. 2:6-7).

In John 6:38-40, Jesus completely identifies with the will of his father:

For I have come down from heaven not to do my will but to do the will of him who sent me. And this is the will of him who sent me, that I shall lose none of all those he has given me, but raise them up at the last day. For my Father's will is that everyone who looks to the Son and believes in him shall have eternal life, and I will raise them up at the last day.

Even more, Jesus understood that his lost brothers and sisters, humanity, were loved so deeply by his father that he (God) could never be satisfied as long as one of his children was without hope of being reconciled to him. Jesus, fully realizing the deep love God has for humanity, also recognized that he alone could satisfy the longing of God to once again be united with his children. It is important to point out that Jesus was consciously aware of who he was and understood his relation to God and that of humanity. Perhaps this was because of his keen consciousness of his own identity and his acceptance that he alone was uniquely and distinctively able to redeem humanity.

Jesus's self-awareness and self-identity spoke directly to his mission and purpose for his life on earth. Because Jesus saw himself, his unique and distinctive relationship to God and man, and embraced his self-awareness and self-identity, he was compelled and propelled to *not consider equality with God something to be used to his own advantage; rather, he made himself nothing by taking the very nature of a servant, being made in human likeness. And being found in appearance as a man, he humbled himself by becoming obedient to death—even death on a cross!* (Phil. 2:6-8).

In like manner, the Scriptures (Phil. 2:5) exhort believers to think and act like Christ in this very way. The mindset to embrace his self-consciousness and self-identity was the mindset by which he accepted and pursued with passion the mission and purpose of God for his life. With this mentality, Jesus willingly gave up his rightly attained seat next to God his Father in glory and was birthed of a woman into humanity. Thereby, he would experience the sights, sounds, tastes, smells, touch, and emotions of life and culture similar to other ordinary Jewish boys from Nazareth.

Jesus's self-awareness and self-identity not only connected to his mission and purpose for life but also served as a navigation device that led him into relationships and experiences that would chart his course from Bethlehem to Calvary. Jesus was born a Jew, raised in Jewish culture, and experienced a life of scarcity from birth, where his family had to work for a living. He was the oldest of several brothers and sisters. Early in his life, Jesus experienced first-hand the threat of violence and trauma of being on the run from the long reaches of government, King Herod. Though he was just a baby, Jesus was hunted like an animal, having to leave his own country to escape attempts on his life. Later, Jesus eventually succumbed, on his own terms, to the hands of the Jewish religious leaders and was publicly crucified on a cross. Nevertheless, he knew his mission and purpose and accomplished it while helping others, teaching them to help themselves and their communities, and inspiring a spirit of generative servant leadership among the communities he lived in and visited.

No doubt, Jesus's early experiences formed opinions in his mind about the oppressed and the oppressors. He served and empathized with the poor, the homeless, the fugitive, the working class, and the rich. He knew the pros and cons of living in fear, with parents who stressed, struggled, and strategized just to keep him alive in his early years.

How can one experience life in this way and learn to love both the oppressed and oppressor? Who seeks to save and minister to both the hurting and the affluent? Jesus could, because he embraced his self-awareness and self-identity, thereby realizing that who he was and who he would become was tied to his heritage and early life experiences.

Embracing self-awareness and self-identity allows us to lift and inspire others! Until we can put on our own masks and wrap our own wounds, what we can do for others is greatly limited. Of necessity, procreant servant leadership begins with helping ourselves through self-awareness and self-identity.

Accepting oneself, makes one fit for the Master's use. This concept is demonstrated with King David in 2 Samuel 7, where David desired to build a house for God, something that many people would probably see as a great and noble gesture, which even the prophet of God, Nathan, initially approved. But as we learned from the story, God did not want David to build him a house because it was not tied to God's purpose for David. To help David and the readers understand this, God used the prophet Nathan to speak to David about his humble beginnings and the mighty hand of God in bringing him to his present state. Apparently, God thought that a lesson in self-awareness and self-identity was necessary in redirecting David.

Self-awareness and self-identity guide our work. As we grow older and gain more experiences and successes, usually the more authority we obtain by virtue of our humanity. Often, many of us want to do something that is meaningful and satisfying with our lives, and many of us want to give back to society and God. Interestingly, the story of David's desire to build a house for God is an Old Testament story that helps us see the significance of self-awareness and self-identity in guiding our decision-making.

In 2 Samuel 7 and 1 Chronicles 17, David was well situated in his life. He lived in a very large and luxurious house, where men protected and served him daily. As king of Israel, he wielded tremendous authority and was respected by those who served him and those whom he served. Even more, his kingdom enjoyed a time of peace, where men were not at war with other nations. It was during this time that David compared his living conditions to those of God and was moved with a strong desire to show his appreciation to God by building Him a house in which to dwell. In his mind, he thought it was not right for him to live in a beautiful house built from fine wood and other precious materials while the house of God lay in a tent. This kind of reasoning would seem rational and appropriate to many people and certainly seemed acceptable to Nathan the prophet. Perhaps David thought that building a big, nice house for God would boost his approval rating among the people, especially since the Israelites showed great reverence for God. Regardless of the reason, David's desire was not part of God's plan for him and was rejected. So, to help David, the Israelites, and those who would read this record to understand why God rejected David's plan, he sent a detailed response to David via the prophet Nathan. In short, the message provided a lesson about the significance of self-awareness and self-identity for servant leaders.

First, David's view of himself was out of focus. In God's message to David, he makes it abundantly clear that David had greatly erred in his thinking about himself in comparison to his God. The passage clearly reveals that God does not simply say no to David's idea, but God sends a sharp rebuke and addresses the fact that David was out of touch with himself. In short, David had forgotten who he was and from where he had come. We know this because God himself sternly reminded David of who he was and from where he had come: self-awareness and self-identity. Here is part of God's message to David:

> *Now then, tell my servant David, "This is what the Lord Almighty says: I took you from the pasture,*

from tending the flock, and appointed you ruler over my people Israel. I have been with you wherever you have gone, and I have cut off all your enemies from before you. Now I will make your name great, like the names of the greatest men on earth."

2 Samuel 7:8-9.

When we fail to correctly understand and embrace who we are, self-awareness and self-identity, it greatly affects our view of others and God. David's view of himself affected his view of who God was to the point that he began to focus on what God needed and how he could help God and thereby gain greater favor.

It appears that David was comparing his life and his progress to that of God, in that his house was great and greatly comfortable, yet "poor" God does not even have a house. Although it is understandable for David to desire to build a beautiful temple for God, it seems as though he had allowed his elevation as king to elevate his self-awareness and self-identity to such a level that he felt the need to lift God by bringing some respect and dignity to God by building a house for him.

Secondly, David's view of God was inconsistent with who God is. Even though it seemed to have been an admirable work, the people and resources were available, the nation was at rest from those who would interrupt the work, and most compelling of all, it was to honor God, yet the answer from God was no. The reason is that God had another purpose for David. He called, delivered, raised, and crowned David for a purpose, which did not include building a house for God. At that time, a house for God wasn't needed, nor was it in God's permissive will for David to build. In response to David's plan to build God a house, God himself said the following to Nathan:

> *"Go and tell my servant David, are you the one to build me a house to dwell in? I have not dwelt in a house from the day I brought the Israelites up out of Egypt to this day. I have been moving from place to place with a tent as my dwelling. Wherever I have moved with all the Israelites, did I ever say to any of their rulers whom I commanded to shepherd my people Israel, 'Why have you not built me a house of cedar?'* (2 Samuel 7:5-7).

> *"The Lord declares to you that the Lord himself will establish a house for you: When your days are over*

and you rest with your ancestors, I will raise up your offspring to succeed you, your own flesh and blood, and I will establish his kingdom" (2 Samuel 7:11b-12).

In the passages above, God clarifies David's role as an earthly king who was placed in position by God to be a helper in carrying out the work and will of God as leader of Israel. In such a position, it's not the servant's role to plan and lead God, especially since he has no way of truly knowing the essence of God or the needs of God, except when God reveals himself. Perhaps it may have been appropriate for David to ask God, "Should I build a house for you?"

Unfortunately, and perhaps unintentionally, David compared his human height and statue and his lavishing luxuries to the physical temple that visually represented the dwelling place of God among his people and decided for himself that God deserved better. And even though one could reasonably make such an assumption, making plans for God without guidance from God seems to reduce the vastness of God to the limitations of the human mind. How can the human mind even conceive the immensity of God to determine a sufficient dwelling place for him, even if it is symbolic?

A servant leader's self-awareness and self-identity are critical for missional focus and fit him or her to serve God by lifting and inspiring others! Helping to heal and lift others requires us to continually anoint and dress our own wounds by connecting with the genealogical and psychological lessons from our past. This requires that we have the right view of who we are and who God is.

Chapter 5
Developing Biblically Based Character

Just as it suggests, developing biblically based character refers to the you that can be advanced, improved, and refined by embracing and practicing values espoused by believers in the Holy Scriptures. The Bible is the inerrant, authoritative, written word of God that *is God-breathed and is useful for teaching, rebuking, correcting and training in righteousness, so that the servant of God may be thoroughly equipped for every good work* (2 Tim. 3:16-17). Two of the well-known values Christians embrace in character development are to love God and to love others. All other values are offsprings of these two directives (Luke 10:27).

Character is the mental and moral values that govern the motives, actions, and decisions of a person. An individual has the mental and physical capacity to choose and embrace the character qualities he or she wants to develop, improve, and refine. For example, it is quite possible for a person who has a cold and stony heart to change the way he thinks and feels about others and to learn to love all humanity deeply and show empathy for those whom he once despised. So while some things about us may never change, our character can be developed, improved, and refined.

The Character Development Process

After returning with his parents from their flight to Egypt, Jesus spent several years growing and developing. Even though he was Jesus, God's only begotten son, full of grace and truth, for our learning and example, he submitted himself to the human growth and development process and grew in wisdom and stature with God and man.

While Jesus was still a child, Mary and Joseph returned to Nazareth with him and raised him among his hometown folk. As a child, Jesus was subject to his parents and grew up in the heritage and traditions of his community. He was observed learning in the temples and actively engaging the doctors and experts of the law. His experience in both Bethlehem and Nazareth was an integral part of who he was humanly and played a great role in his view of himself, others, and his ministry. Frequently, as an adult,

Jesus taught using parables, which may have been reflective of his own upbringing and life experiences.

Jesus was not bound, but guided and liberated by his self-consciousness and self-identity regarding his humanity. These experiences spoke expressly to him about the need for ministry and the call and purpose God had on his life. Because he embraced himself and his story, he could identify with others like him, enabling his desire to help them and teach them to help themselves and one another.

Prior to announcing his own call into ministry, Jesus spent time growing and developing physically, embracing his own childhood and humanity, and learning and practicing the Holy Scriptures. Jesus was about thirty years of age when he began to call his disciples to follow him as their teacher. Although there may be many reasons why Jesus didn't announce his ministry or call his followers earlier, one thought that arises from his example is that it allowed him to demonstrate to humanity the need to develop, improve, and refine one's own character prior to leading others in character development.

Identify the Character Traits You Want to Master

Although there are many character traits, identifying those you wish to internalize and embrace tightly is a decision you must make. Everyone does not embrace the same positive character traits with the same level of commitment to practicing them. Even professed, born-again believers may differ in the character traits they choose to tightly embrace. One thing we have learned from biblical days is that morality cannot be legislated effectively. At the end of the day, the level of commitment one has to embracing specific character traits greatly depends on how deeply the individual values the traits and how devoted he is to allowing them to transform his life. Perhaps this is one reason that pastors, evangelists, and other church leaders all over America can teach about love during Bible studies, worship services, Bible conferences, and other spirit-filled events that take place weekly throughout the nation, yet there is widespread hatred, violence, and criminal activity in many local communities nationwide. The diverse views about which character traits are most important and how they are applied to others may help explain why it is so difficult to gain widespread support from local churches on many crucial moral issues that face our society. So how does one determine the most important character traits to embrace? For this book, that answer lies within the pages of the Holy Scriptures, the Bible.

It is a common practice for people seeking to become successful, respected citizens to look to coaches or mentors to emulate. The upside to this is that you can have a model to emulate and aspire to be like. On the downside, often the people we admire and aspire to be like also have character flaws. But be mindful that we should not judge others too harshly, because all humans have shortcomings and vulnerabilities. Yet, we are called to love and serve one another after the example of Christ. Consider King David, as great as he was, a man that God himself proclaimed to be a man after God's heart. Yet David took the wife of his servant, Uriah, and slept with and impregnated her while Uriah was fighting to protect King David and his country. Even worse, when David was afraid that he would be exposed, he had Uriah killed. Although David later repented and served God faithfully, it may baffle the ordinary citizen to understand how God could not only restore David but also promised to build David a great lineage through whom God's only human son, Jesus, would be born, thereby establishing the kingdom of David forever, through Christ. So, this David, who had other human flaws, is the example that God lifts to humanity as being a man after the heart of God. In short, this says to us that God forgives and uses men with flaws.

Consequently, looking at others and admiring their godly qualities is okay; however, it is kind of sad to observe a person seeking to help others to build and develop in an area where they themselves are failing miserably. Now, this doesn't mean that a person cannot serve and accomplish great work while battling his own personal weaknesses (inner struggles) or weaknesses related to their skills and abilities in an area of ministry, but it does imply that effectively helping others over hurdles that trip you up requires a certain level of mastery. For example, if you are teaching students how to live a life of fidelity to their spouse but you privately engage in watching pornographic images with ungodly thoughts, unfortunately, your ability to effectively guide others in developing singleness of heart for their spouse will be limited. Even though you may lecture wonderfully and inspire many, your own limitation in sharing with students how you succeeded and maintained your area of marital fidelity will be impeded.

In sports, some athletic coaches have never played the game professionally, yet they have become very successful in coaching teams to experience high levels of success. However, this does not hold true with character coaches. You see, character coaches are lifetime examples to their students and must continue to master the character trait they teach because we shall be judged by the same standards and shall "receive the greater condemnation" (James 3:1). So looking to others, aside from Jesus, as an example of the perfect model for servant leadership is not practical. For this reason, I turn to the Bible for an example, because it is the only source I know that is time-tested.

The Bible is a source that many in society have turned to for many years. Although some people do not consider themselves to be devout followers of the Christian faith, they have come to respect the Bible as a valued source for identifying character traits that people should embrace and practice. As diverse as society has become, still many people across America gather for weekly Bible study and

Sunday worship to learn about Jesus and further develop a biblically based character. The Bible is said to contain the divinely written and inspired word of God and exclaims that "All Scripture is God-breathed and is useful for teaching, rebuking, correcting and training in righteousness, so that the servant of God may be thoroughly equipped for every good work (2 Tim. 3:16). Additionally, I have found the Bible to be a very reliable source for providing guidance for building character.

However, even when one turns to the Bible, the list of godly character traits can be very long. Since they are all important, shouldn't we just embrace them all equally? This is a great question and one that Jesus responded to when he was asked which law was the most important for men to follow. He answered by identifying love as being the most important character trait and went on to say that loving God and others is the greatest demonstration of that character trait.

One important aspect of servant leadership is helping one's self. This applies to character building as well. Once a servant leader develops in himself the character he wishes to build in others, then he can effectively demonstrate the character qualities, rather than verbalizing them only. An inspiring quote attributed to Mahatma Gandhi says, *Be the change you want to see in the world.* The saying is powerful and is one that Gandhi sought to emulate in his own life before he took up the mantle as a world-renowned civil rights leader. Even as he moved into the prominence of his role, he actively studied and practiced the character values he espoused in others. In his autobiography, Gandhi shares his early resolve and ongoing struggles to build and maintain the character he wished to pass on to others, including his oppressors and enemies.

Loving Others as We Love Ourselves

As Jesus responded to the question about which was the greatest commandment, he said that we should love God with all our heart and that we should love our neighbors as we love ourselves (Matt. 22:39). This verse gives us the expectation and measuring tool by which we should love others, which is determined by how much we love ourselves. The indication is that it is normal for people to love and care for themselves. It is actually a bad thing for people to grossly neglect their own health and happiness in the name of helping others, because self-love makes us fit to love others.

By loving ourselves, we show appreciation and acceptance for who we are as children of God. This is an important step toward being able to express the highest form of love that we can show others, which is to be their servant. When we serve others, we show the fullness of Jesus's love toward humanity. We show humility, compassion, empathy, and esteem for others above ourselves. These are the qualities that compelled Jesus to move from his seat at the right hand of God in glory and to give his life to serve people who were clearly out of fellowship with God the father and not on his level of righteousness. Here we see vividly the love of Jesus demonstrated in his highest act of service.

Jesus was the embodiment of love for himself, his father, and those whom he served. He understood the need to love and care for himself adequately, as self-care enabled him to regain physical strength and engage daily in prayer with God in a time of solitude, thereby refreshing him for the journey of helping others and teaching them to help themselves.

Refreshing oneself by gaining proper rest is an important part of self-care. In Genesis 2:1-2, God shares something with us about himself that is simple yet quite amazing. He shares with us that after his first six days of work, as recorded in Genesis, he rested, he took a break to revitalize himself. Now, it is quite obvious from what we know about God that it is quite unlikely that God was tired, since "he . . . neither slumber nor sleep" (Ps. 121:4). Nevertheless, God not only reveals to us that he rested, but he later instituted a weekly day of rest for all of humanity.

So why did God want us to know that he took a day to rest? Well, one thing that stands out in my mind is that rest is appropriate for anyone who has worked. Anyone who has toiled, labored, strove, or exerted energy needs time to rest. It also says to us that work is good, is how God intends for us to oversee his creation, and is how we should provide for our own needs and those of others who depend on us.

The Bible says that God created all of his creation in six consecutive days, and when it was done, complete, and finished, he retreated and rested. Another reason God may have rested is to highlight the need to celebrate success. He not only taught humanity the need to work to complete a task and the need to rest, but also how to celebrate a job well done. The celebration was a time to retreat and enjoy the present success. "There is a time for everything, and a season for every activity under the heaven" (Ecc. 3:1), and the celebration is a good reason to rest (Eckel 2013).

The Process for Building Biblically Based Character

Procreant servant leaders base their process for creating biblically based character on the life of Jesus and his relationship with his disciples. The process below includes five broad categories depicting steps that Jesus may have followed as he transformed the character of his twelve disciples in preparation for ministry. These categories are not intended to provide a detailed step-by-step guide to character development. However, they provide institutions with parameters that help guide others in the preparation of procreant servant leaders and institutions in the direction Jesus took to develop character in his disciples. These parameters may be thought of in terms of Kenneth Blanchard's analogy of the function of river banks.

Blanchard says that *a river without banks is a large puddle.* So just as river banks help to contain and give direction to the flow of the river, lessons from Jesus's relationship with his disciples provide the banks that guide the process for creating procreant servant leaders. The following categories are derived from reflecting on the life of Jesus in relationship to his twelve disciples as he prepared them to serve others. The categories serve as the parameters for developing character in procreant servant leaders:

- Jesus **invited** his disciples to follow him.
- Jesus **taught** them by precepts and examples.
- Jesus **engaged** them in character-building work.
- Jesus **modeled** for them what biblically based character looks like.
- Jesus **empowered and released** them to do the work.

One important observation in the process is that Jesus is the outright leader. He calls his followers, teaches them, engages them in character-building work, models what biblically based character looks like, and, finally, empowers and releases them for the work. You may notice that Jesus is the subject of each statement and the doer of the action in each sentence, thereby making him the principal player in fostering the character development of his twelve disciples. Let's dig a little deeper as we take a glimpse at each of the five parameters.

1. Jesus invited his disciples to follow him. Access to Jesus's character-development program was by invitation. This is a significant point and should not be downplayed as coincidental or inconsequential. I believe that there are many reasons for this, but here are just a few:

- A person can only effectively mentor a few people. The type of mentoring Jesus engaged in with his disciples was an all-day, every day commitment. This does not mean that he was physically with each of them every hour of the day, but he did devote time frequently to engaging them and opening his life as a model for them.
- The mentor and mentee must be the right fit. The relationship must be right or God ordained. Jesus knew those whom God had given him, and he was careful to only call them, because they (he and his disciples) were the right fit for one another.

- One key to knowing that the mentor-mentee is in a right-fit relationship is that the mentee heeds the call and submits to the instruction of the mentor, and the mentor is loving, accommodating, and apt to teach his mentee, especially when the mentee falls short.

2. Jesus taught them by precepts and examples. The teachings of Jesus were practical and by principle. He taught them basic values and guidelines for prosperous communal living and the advancement of the kingdom of God. He frequently used relatable stories and proverbs to ensure that the disciples grasped the concepts and ideals being taught. Jesus seemed to work diligently to make his lessons practical. He taught his disciples to think deeply about life by reflecting on and actively applying biblical principles in problem-solving. Jesus often used parables and the Socratic method of teaching to engage his disciples and to get them to dive deeper into their reflection and understanding of biblical truths. Also, he placed them in positions where they would have to exercise their knowledge and faith to accomplish some ministry missions and experiential learning.

3. Jesus engaged them in character-building work. A key part of the mentoring process was practicing the lessons taught. Jesus involved his disciples in character-building

work by sending them out to serve without him and by having them assist him in ministering to others. For example, he used his disciples to help serve the hungry and give guidance to those gathered to hear him.

4. Jesus modeled for them what biblically based character looks like. Probably the most important part of the character-development process is that the mentee has an opportunity to see what biblically based character looks like in action. Teaching, providing examples, and practicing are all invaluable components of the character-development process. However, seeing Jesus serve and deal with people of various psychological, social, emotional, and religious backgrounds and what biblically based character looks like under the intense pressure of his private Gethsemane prayer and the excruciating pain and shame of the cross were paramount experiences for the disciples' character-development process. These experiences of a biblically based character modeled by Jesus would guide and inspire the disciples as they became martyrs for the cause of Christ.

5. Jesus empowered and released them to do the work. It was ten days after Jesus had ascended into heaven that he sent the Holy Spirit to empower the eleven disciples (minus Judas) and others who were waiting with them.

This seminal event marked the day his disciples were to begin making disciples of men and displaying their biblically based character.

Jesus's example gives parameters for procreant servant leaders and institutions to create other servant leaders who will help themselves, help others, help others to help themselves, and inspire a spirit of generative servant leadership in the communities where they live and work.

Chapter 6
Building Capacity in Others

In the context of an individual servant leader, capacity refers to the ableness of a person to help him or herself, help others, and inspire a spirit of servant leadership in the communities where he or she lives and works. An individual's capacity or ableness is measured based on the quantity or quality of one's gifts, skills, and talents, their preparedness and willingness to serve, and their commitment to being accountable and responsible for faithful service to humanity.

The capacity is relative to the individual because everyone does not have the same individual capacity. Studying the model of Jesus in relation to his twelve disciples and following the corresponding parameters of procreant servant leadership for building capacity in others are key to understanding the process.

The Capacity-Building Process
In a broad aspect, Jesus's program for building the individual capacity of his twelve disciples seemed to follow a pattern that included selecting the right students,

building the right foundation, and engaging them in the right experiential learning. Below is a concise description of each component of the capacity-building process, based on the life of Jesus in relationship to his twelve disciples. This model is similar to the one we used above to discuss parameters for the character-building process.

1. **Selecting the right students:** The *right students* refers to connecting the right mentees (disciples) with the right mentor (teacher). This is of utmost significance because both the mentee and mentor must be committed to the process and have high regard for one another. Remember that while Jesus ministered to the masses, he only mentored a small group of disciples, and before choosing them, he went out to a mountainside and spent the night praying to God (Luke 6:12-26). Here are a few points to ponder about the relationship:

- Jesus ministered to the masses, but he only discipled (mentored) a few followers—commonly referred to as the twelve.
- Jesus's disciples were a gift to him by God (John 17:12; Luke 6:12-26).
- Jesus himself called his disciples (mentees) to follow him, and they willingly did so.

- Jesus was the outright leader (teacher), and his disciples were expected to willingly engage in the learning process.
- The disciples seemed to be inquisitive and practical; they were not blind followers.
- The disciples represented ordinary people with a variety of backgrounds and personalities.

Pertinent Points

- All believers are called to be servants, but not all are chosen to be procreant servant leaders.
- Procreant servant leaders may minister to the masses, but they can only mentor a few.
- The discipleship (mentorship) principle is built on foundational and liberating truths.

2. **The right foundation:** Jesus's teachings were transformative because they were based on foundational truths that liberated people personally and relationally in their human and spiritual lives. Transformational education is the ability to introduce and sustain ideological change by sharing what you know with others in such a way that they embrace the knowledge as truth and allow it to change their lives. Knowing your individual and

relational truths, humanly and spiritually, is important to forming the right foundation on which to build and expand your capacity to serve others.

Earthly truths refer to individual and relational facts and realities that helps you to understand who you are and how you made it to where you are, the particulars of your journey. They are integral to your being, heritage, and purpose. Good or bad, happy or sad, desirable or not, these truths have been a part of your growth and development process and, in some cases, may greatly enhance or inhibit your future.

Individual facts refer to those foundational truths that are specific to the person. They may include your DNA, parents, sex, skin color, hair color and texture, and unique individual experiences. These things happened independently of your input, choice, or effort; nonetheless, they are uniquely you.

Relational facts refer to who you are in relation to other human beings (socially, economically, emotionally, psychologically, etc.). Like the individual truths, many relational facts and realities were not by choice or consent. You did not choose your parent's occupation, their friends, the neighborhood in which you were reared, or the heritage and traditions of your culture. Yet these relational facts and realities connect you to an invaluable part of who you are.

Earthly Foundational Truths
Your knowledge of many of your earthly foundational truths depends on what you learn about your story from your family, ancestors, and society. These stories help you affirm who you are individually and relationally. The stories help you know more about yourself and, in a very real way, help inform and inspire your purpose in life. Additionally, they provide a rallying point when you face extreme adversity.

Sharing of earthly foundational truths starts at home with teaching your children who they are and instilling in them the manners and morals you believe are important. Parents should help assimilate their children into the life they wish for them to lead as adults. They should invest time and resources and give them space to learn and grow into servant leaders who will help lift their communities and inspire a spirit of generative servant leadership in the communities where they live and work. Perhaps the most effective and widely known story for transforming the lives of people is found in the pages of the Holy Scriptures. From Genesis to Revelation, the Bible presents a story about God, his people, and his plan for them.

An Old Testament example of the significance of knowing and embracing one's earthly foundational truths is found in Daniel 1, where King Nebuchadnezzar gave instructions for assimilating Hebrew people from Judah into Babylon. It appears that the king's main concern beyond their physical fitness and mental capacity was their ability to become loyal subjects in the king's service. So he made learning the Chaldean language and literature a prerequisite to their standing before his presence and being brought into his service. Perhaps the king felt that if the captives had an understanding of the Chaldean language and literature, they would become loyal subjects to the king and his service.

When people fully embrace the language and stories of a place, they are more likely to fit into and become loyal to the culture. At that point, others don't have to tell them how and what to think. It becomes a part of their thinking process. Consequently, "they" become "we."

Learning the literature tells the story of what is good, acceptable, and valuable to a people. The eyes of their understanding become glazed by what the literature shows to be important and protected. The writer controls the narrative, and when you base your truth upon the facts and fiction of the story, you automatically begin to think how the writer thinks, solve problems like the writer does, and appraise beauty and value as the writer does.

Spiritual Foundational Truths

Spiritual foundational truths for those of the Christian faith often depend on what you learn about who God is from your family and communal life. The stories and testimonies of others help affirm your faith and traditions. Participation in biblical training programs and activities provides lifelong experiences that are likely to positively influence your choice or style of worship.

However, in the Christian faith, the individual experience with Jesus leads one to the salvation experience, which is gained by accepting as truth that Jesus is the son of God and the savior of the world, and confessing him as the savior. This is the central truth upon which the Christian faith is founded.

"If you hold to my teaching, you are really my disciples. Then you will know the truth, and the truth will "make you free" (John 8:31-32 KJV). This reality is an individual responsibility, which connects the believer personally to God the creator as a son or daughter. This then makes the believer, relationally, a part of the family of God and entitles him or her to all of the privileges of being a son or daughter.

3. The Right Experiential Learning

People are generally born with gifts and talents and with some capacity to serve others; however, increasing or maximizing an individual's capacity as a servant leader involves a process. The process Jesus used included experiential learning by engaging in the work of serving and leading others while under the watchful eye of the teacher.

A great example of expanding individual capacity to serve is illustrated in a parable given by Jesus in Matthew 25:14-30:

The Parable of the Bags of Gold

> *Again, it will be like a man going on a journey, who called his servants and entrusted his wealth to them. To one he gave five bags of gold, to another two bags, and to another one bag, each according to his ability. Then he went on his journey. The man who had received five bags of gold went at once and put his money to work and gained five bags more. So also, the one with two bags of gold gained two more. But the man who had received one bag went off, dug a hole in the ground and hid his master's money. After a long time the master of those servants returned and settled accounts with them. The man who had received five bags of gold brought the other five. 'Master,' he said, 'you entrusted me with five bags of gold. See, I have gained five more.' His master replied, 'Well done, good and faithful servant! You have been faithful with a few things; I will put you in charge of many things. Come and share your master's happiness!' The man with two bags of gold also came. 'Master,' he said, 'you entrusted me with two bags of gold; see, I have gained two more.'*

"His master replied, 'Well done, good and faithful servant! You have been faithful with a few things; I will put you in charge of many things. Come and share your master's happiness!' Then the man who had received one bag of gold came. 'Master,' he said, 'I knew that you are a hard man, harvesting where you have not sown and gathering where you have not scattered seed. 25 So I was afraid and went out and hid your gold in the ground. See, here is what belongs to you.' His master replied, 'You wicked, lazy servant! So you knew that I harvest where I have not sown and gather where I have not scattered seed? Well then, you should have put my money on deposit with the bankers, so that when I returned I would have received it back with interest. So take the bag of gold from him and give it to the one who has ten bags. For whoever has will be given more, and they will have an abundance. Whoever does not have, even what they have will be taken from them. And throw that worthless servant outside, into the darkness, where there will be weeping and gnashing of teeth.'

Observations from the Parable

1. People have various capacity levels. Consequently, all are not equipped to handle the same level of responsibility.
2. One should embrace who he is and serve to the best of his ability.
3. People should seek to increase their capacity, not just maintain it.
4. Rewards are not measured by the effort or success of others.
5. Attitude affects performance.

The Essence of Expanding Capacity!

Your success expands your capability and capacity to serve.

The parable gives us revelatory knowledge that is practically and empirically based:

1. All can serve and all can expand. The master gave talents (responsibility) according to the capacity of the individual to effectively manage and grow it/them. This is significant because it means that the master knew how much each of the servants was capable of successfully managing. Yet all were given tasks regardless of their capacity levels.

2. All are expected to expand, measured quantifiably and/or empirically. The master expected the servants to make full use of the talent(s) by working diligently to bring forth an increase in proportion to the servant's capacity. Therefore, their progress was measured accordingly.
3. When the workers increased their talents (gifts), the master gave them more of their own and more to work with, thereby expanding their capacity to handle and make more.
4. At the end of the parable, the reward was for faithfulness, and therefore both were rewarded the same gift – **I will make you ruler over many things**.
5. Because the individual with one talent failed to fully use it, his capacity did not expand and he lost what was given to him. The unproductive servant was rejected and removed.

Chapter 7
Inspiring Others to Serve

For a three-year period, Jesus ministered to multitudes, but fascinatingly, he only mentored twelve, who had been chosen after a night of prayer. Interestingly, they remained with him for the duration of his earthly ministry and were extraordinarily successful. Only the son of perdition, Judas, was lost. For this reason, we will look to Jesus's relationship with his eleven remaining disciples as a model for inspiring servant leaders who serve and lift others and their communities perpetually.

Jesus's model for inspiring the eleven to serve and lift their communities included providing them with a **clear mission, authentic authority, and unlimited power** to minister. The model was demonstrated by Jesus as he ministered to and mentored his disciples prior to his death, but it was after Jesus's resurrection that he commissioned them into the service, and it was following his ascension that he empowered and released the eleven to minister and lift communities throughout the world. The commissioning "ceremony" is plainly captured in Matthew

28:16-20, and their empowerment is vividly described in Acts 1:4-8 and Acts 2:1-14.

Great Commission
Matthew 28:16-20

Then the eleven disciples went to Galilee, to the mountain where Jesus had told them to go. When they saw him, they worshiped him; but some doubted. Then Jesus came to them and said, "All authority in heaven and on earth has been given to me. Therefore go and make disciples of all nations, baptizing them in the name of the Father and of the Son and of the Holy Spirit, and teaching them to obey everything I have commanded you. And surely I am with you always, to the very end of the age."

The Day of Pentecost
Acts 1:4-8

On one occasion, while he was eating with them, he gave them this command: "Do not leave Jerusalem, but wait for the gift my Father promised, which you have heard me speak about. For John baptized with water, but in a few days you will be baptized with the Holy Spirit. . . . You will receive power when the Holy Spirit comes on you; and you will be my witnesses in Jerusalem, and in all Judea and Samaria, and to the ends of the earth."

Acts 2:1, 4, 14

When the day of Pentecost came, they were all together in one place. . . . All of them were filled with the Holy Spirit and began to speak in other tongues as the Spirit enabled them. . . . Then Peter stood up with the Eleven, raised his voice and addressed the crowd.

Here is a brief description of what is meant by clear mission, authentic authority, and unlimited power in this context:

1. **Clear mission** refers to the directive that Jesus gave to the eleven disciples to "Go and make disciples of all nations, baptizing them in the name of the Father and of the Son and of the Holy Spirit, and teaching them to obey everything I have commanded you."
2. **Authentic authority** refers to the legitimate right bestowed on the eleven disciples by Jesus himself to invoke his name (Father, Son, and Holy Spirit) when making and baptizing other disciples.
3. **Unlimited power** refers to the disciples being filled with the Holy Spirit, thereby enabling them to carry out their

assigned mission at home and abroad.

The Commissioning Ceremony

First, let's take a closer look at the commissioning event, which occurred in Galilee after Jesus's resurrection. During the commissioning event, two important things took place: Jesus gave a clear mission to the disciples and gave them the authority to invoke his name in making disciples. These two directives continue to be foundational for inspiring and guiding the church's work more than 2,100 years later. Even though there are many Christian denominations with varying worship styles and activities, the principal motivation that inspires their evangelistic and teaching ministries is couched in the directive to "go" and make disciples in Jesus's name.

I believe that the time, place, and conducting of the commissioning ceremony was intentional and solemn. Not everyone was invited to observe, nor was every follower invited to be commissioned. This ceremony was for those who were prepared, who had completed the three-year mentoring program with Jesus and were ready to accept the mission and authority to carry out the work. So while other disciples may very well have been there, we only see evidence that Jesus summoned his eleven disciples to Galilee to meet him following his resurrection.

According to Matthew's gospel, following Jesus's resurrection, he sent his eleven disciples a message to meet him in Galilee, at which time Jesus gave them the mission and authority to go into their communities and throughout the world serving and lifting up people. Here are some particulars about the mission and conferring of authority.

Particulars about the Mission: While there are many important points to be made about the mission Jesus gave to the disciples following his resurrection, here are a few salient points to consider:

➤ All eleven disciples had been summoned by Jesus to receive the mission.
➤ All were present to receive the mission.
➤ All were prepared by Jesus to carry out the mission.
➤ All willingly received the mission.
➤ Each was responsible for advancing the mission.

It is important to recognize that the mission to carry the gospel was not given to community leaders, politicians, social groups, activists, entertainers, or secular business owners, nor were nonbelievers commanded by Jesus to provide support for the ministry. The marvel is that it appears that only a few believers heartily embrace the mission from generation to generation, yet it continues to be carried mightily and serves as a perpetual light amidst darkness and unbelief.

Particulars about the Conferring of Authority: In addition to receiving a clear mission, the disciples were given authority to invoke the name of Jesus when carrying out the mission of the church. At the time of the Galilee meeting, Jesus had completed his own mission of suffering, shedding his blood, and dying for the sin of humanity; being victorious over death, hell, and the grave; being resurrected by God the Father; and receiving all authority in heaven and on earth (Matt. 28:18).

Here are a few salient points about the conferring of authority.

> Jesus himself had legitimately received "all" power and authority. This meant that he not only had authority over everything but also had the legal right to confer authority upon others.

> Conferring of authority. This gave the eleven disciples the legal right to invoke Jesus's name, with the assurance that the full weight of Jesus's authority and power guarantees that those who receive Christ and are baptized will be saved.

These points alone underscore the significance of the commissioning as an intentional and solemn event where prepared believers were directed to carry out the mission to evangelize and receive souls in the name of Jesus.

Power to Serve

Ten days after Jesus's ascension into heaven, the book of Acts describes the momentous account of the day of Pentecost, as written by Luke. The word Pentecost means fiftieth. There had been fifty days since Jesus's resurrection. Forty of those days, Jesus spent appearing to the eleven and many other of his disciples, and during the forty days, Jesus commissioned the eleven. However, he commanded that they not leave Jerusalem, but wait until they had received the power of the Holy Spirit. This power would live within them and give them the wisdom and strength they needed to effectively carry out the mission of Jesus. While some use the words *authority* and *power* interchangeably, I prefer to distinguish between them as follows:

- **Authority** is the legal right to do something or give directives. It is a term that operates out of the legitimacy of the office or place it holds. It is often exercised by issuing directives or orders.

- **Power** is the ability or might to do something or make something happen. The power of the Holy Spirit not only physically strengthens us, but gives us wisdom, knowledge, understanding, discernment, guidance, boldness, favor, warning, and protection.

Example of authority: A local judge may issue an order for a guilty person to serve a day in jail. Because of his office, the people in the community have given the judge the legal right to adjudicate and issue orders. As long as he is in his office, his orders are legitimate and have the backing of law enforcement agencies.

Example of power: When a person is ordered by a judge to spend a day in jail, law enforcement personnel take control of the situation and exercise the power of their office to place the person in handcuffs and carry him to jail. They have the means to physically carry out the orders of the judge.

Scriptural Example: Jesus Clears the Temple Courts, John 2:13-18.
When it was almost time for the Jewish Passover, Jesus went up to Jerusalem. In the temple courts he found people selling cattle, sheep and doves, and others sitting at tables exchanging money. So he made a whip out of cords, and drove all from the temple courts, both sheep and cattle; he scattered the coins of the money changers and overturned their tables. To those who sold doves he said, "Get these out of here! Stop turning my Father's house into a market!" His disciples remembered that it is written: "Zeal for your house will consume me." The Jews then responded to him, "What sign can you show us to prove your authority to do all this?"

Authority: In his office (position) as the son of God, Jesus acted legitimately. Psalm 69:9 says, "For zeal for your house consumes me, and the insults of those who insult you fall on me." In verse 17 of the scripture above Jesus's "disciples remembered that it is written: 'Zeal for your house will consume me.'"

Power: Being led by his passion and the power of the Holy Spirit, Jesus took action and "made a whip out of cords, and drove all from the temple courts."

Note: The Jews in this passage were legalists, so their question to Jesus was not, "Why did you do this?" but, *"What sign can you show us to prove your authority to do all this?"* Perhaps they were asking this question because without proper authority, they could accuse him of a crime and have him punished. This example shows us how authority and power are interconnected and how one without the other is incomplete.

Here are some salient points about the Holy Spirit:
➢ Each of the disciples needed the Holy Spirit, despite having been given a clear mission by Jesus and authority to invoke his name in disciple making.

➢ Each of the disciples was filled with the Holy Spirit individually. This is important because it indicates that he ministers and lives within them individually.

➢ All of Jesus's disciples spoke in tongues (other languages) as the Spirit enabled them. This seemed to serve as evidence to others of the gift within the disciples.

➢ The Holy Spirit was released to each of them as a gift from Jesus. He (the Holy Spirit) cannot be purchased or earned.

➢ They all had to wait for him. He came upon them at an appointed time.

Inspiring others to serve their communities and society effectively as procreant servant leaders after the example of Jesus in relation to his disciples requires having a clear mission, authority, and power. All three of these elements were necessary in that Jesus would not release his disciples to begin making other disciples until they had all three. In this way, they would be able to go all over the world without his physical presence and still be able to carry out the mission of the church with authority and power from generation to generation, perpetually. This is the miraculous testament of the church.

Chapter 8
Lifting Our Communities!

The way to lift our communities so they are safe, caring, economically stable, self-sustaining places to live is to create procreant servant leaders *from our communities, for our communities*. The need for capable leaders who understand the language and literature of the people in the communities where they live and work and are committed to helping them and inspiring a spirit of generative servant leadership among them is the most effective way to lift our communities.

The need for servant leadership did not stop with the commissioning and empowering of Jesus's eleven disciples. As the work of the church progressed, so did the need for help from servant leaders, who dedicated themselves to helping others and inspiring a spirit of generative servant leadership in the communities where they lived and worked. Acts chapter 6:1-7 provides a great example of recognizing and filling our communities' need for servant leaders.

Expanding Servant Leadership Beyond the Apostles

In those days when the number of disciples was increasing, the Hellenistic Jews among them complained against the Hebraic Jews because their widows were being overlooked in the daily distribution of food. So the Twelve gathered all the disciples together and said, "It would not be right for us to neglect the ministry of the word of God in order to wait on tables. Brothers and sisters, choose seven men from among you who are known to be full of the Spirit and wisdom. We will turn this responsibility over to them and will give our attention to prayer and the ministry of the word." This proposal pleased the whole group. They chose Stephen, a man full of faith and of the Holy Spirit; also Philip, Procorus, Nicanor, Timon, Parmenas, and Nicolas from Antioch, a convert to Judaism. They presented these men to the apostles, who prayed and laid their hands on them. So the word of God spread. The number of disciples in Jerusalem increased rapidly, and a large number of priests became obedient to the faith (Acts 6:1-7).

Here, the apostles recognized and operated in their call to be servant leaders. They may be considered first-generational servant leaders and pioneers of the early church. They had been mentored, empowered, and sent forth by Jesus to help others and teach them to help themselves, as well as those in the communities in which they lived and worked. The apostles were seasoned servants recruited and trained by Jesus himself, who had directed the apostles on at least two occasions in the feeding of large crowds. They had served under Jesus and were presently serving the people, both spiritually and physically. Jesus had helped his disciples to embrace self-awareness and self-identity, develop biblically based character, and build their capacity to serve others, and he inspired them to serve their communities and the world.

But now the need had come to expand the call for servant leadership.

Secondly, the apostles recognized the cry of the poor and their need for assistance to effectively and adequately meet the growing demand for help. Here are a few salient points about the needy in the passage and in society:

- They existed despite living in an economically thriving community.
- The proper distribution of resources, not the lack of resources, seems to be the main issue.
- The believers in the community had a duty to care for the needs of their poor.

In an effort to effectively and appropriately respond to the cry of their poor, the apostles helped the community of believers develop a system to ensure that the needs of the poor were **systemically** addressed.

The essential task was that of creating procreant servant leaders from among the community of believers who would ensure that the poor were receiving proper care and support, generatively. In this situation, there did not appear to be a lack of resources among the community of believers, but there was a problem with ensuring a certain population received their share of food and care.

Is it possible that even today, many believers are living in poverty amidst a community of abundance?

Points to Ponder

Procreant servant leaders do more than help people. They help people to help themselves. In this parable, the disciples ensured the community had a system in place to adequately and perpetually address the main issue: unfair food distribution.

If systemic change is to effectively occur community-wide, there must be servant leaders on the ground in every community and neighborhood making sure that the community resources are fairly and equitably distributed among believers as intended.

The system must be generative, which requires continuous preparation and empowering of procreant servant leaders, *from our communities, for our communities.*

Thirdly, the apostles developed and implemented a plan to commission and empower more servant leaders. The plan was simple, and the process included calling or selecting prepared men and giving them a clear mission, authority, and power to carry out their mission.

The Selection of Servant Leaders

The disciples gave criteria and processes for selecting the leaders who would serve the community of believers. The criteria included selecting men who were filled with the Holy Spirit and served with integrity among the people with whom they lived and worked. In other words, they were observed to have demonstrated a level of success in their personal and professional lives. Allowing the community of believers to look among themselves and identify the candidates may have served as a method of character screening and a vote of confidence in those selected. Here are some of the other characteristics they looked for:

- **Clear mission:** The mission called for the leaders to use their administrative skills and leadership abilities to devise, implement, and oversee a plan that would ensure that the Hellenistic Jews received an adequate portion of food during the daily distribution, while ensuring the community continued to prosper.

- **Authentic authority:** Carrying out the mission required the leaders to have the legal right to enact and carry out rules and procedures to ensure that the poor and needy received adequate food for daily needs. The authority for the selected servant leaders came from two bodies: the community of believers and the disciples. The disciples instructed the community of believers "to choose seven men from among you who are known to be full of the Spirit and wisdom" (Acts 6:3), and the twelve disciples would subsequently "turn this responsibility" (Acts 6:3) for overseeing the distribution of food to the seven new disciples. The commissioning included an event where the apostles prayed over, anointed, and laid hands on the seven as a formal imbuing of authority to act in the assigned positions.

- **Power within:** Following the commissioning ceremony, which included providing the leaders with a clear mission and authentic authority, the power of the Spirit-filled leaders was demonstrated in the enormous success of their work: "The number of disciples in Jerusalem increased rapidly, and a large number of priests became obedient to the faith" (Acts 6:7).

Preparing and Empowering Procreant Servant Leaders for Today!

Is There a Need?

Just a few weeks ago, I was contacted by an employer who was looking for young people who wanted to become computer technicians. No prior experience or higher education was needed. He was willing to hire them as they were and pay them as they trained on the job. His only requirements were that they showed up for work when they were supposed to and were willing to follow instructions. This was exciting to me, and I agreed to look out for good candidates to recommend to him. But as I thought, it became quite a task to find young people who were dependable and willing to work. Even though I know many young people who need to work and have the physical ability, unfortunately, the ones that I could think of who were reliable and willing to work were already working or pursuing other career paths. Perhaps this is relevant to Jesus's statement, *The harvest is plentiful, but the laborers are few* (Matt. 9:27).

The need and desire for good workers with servant hearts is priceless. Many churches, communities, and employers will pay handsomely to find workers who are honest, reliable, responsible, respectful, kind, and willing to work with a servant's heart.

Many communities still have a great need for access to technology, digital equity, better-paying jobs, quality educational resources, adequate healthcare, and other essential long overdue resources; however, providing these resources without investing in committed and capable procreant servant leaders for every community and neighborhood is likely to have little sustainable positive change on the deteriorating conditions in our communities. The availability of resources in America does not seem to be the number one problem in our communities, nor is access our greatest impediment. However, I submit to you that the pressing need is for capable and committed procreant servant leaders on the ground in every community and neighborhood, who will ensure that community resources are fairly and equitably distributed among believers as intended and help to lift and inspire a spirit of generative servant leadership in the communities where they live and work.

Understanding the Problem

In many cases, the lack of procreant servant leaders in communities is due to a condition that I call *community talent drain syndrome*. This phenomenon may be described as a systemic condition, especially pronounced in small rural cities and towns, caused by the systematic removal of the best and brightest academically minded, athletically inclined, aesthetically appealing, and socially entertaining people from a community on a routine basis.

Unfortunately, for more than fifty years, community talent drain syndrome
has wreaked havoc on the many small Black Belt communities, which are experiencing a steady, prolonged population decline, exacerbated by high poverty, high crime, academically low-performing schools, and limited access to technology, among other challenges.

In one example, community talent drain syndrome occurs regularly using a
systematic approach. It involves recruiters who solicit and garner the widespread support of high school coaches, teachers, advisors, counselors, political leaders, etc., who enthusiastically participate in the talent drain process by

encouraging their students to enroll in schools or training programs or join organizations that cart them away with the promise of preparing them to become productive and successful members of society.

Usually, with lots of fanfare, the parents, teachers, and community leaders send off their most valuable resources, with little expectation that they will return to live in or near their hometowns. Sadly, most of the students don't return. Instead, they find employment in other cities or towns, thereby using their talents and resources to grow other communities.

The Solution

Even though there is a real need for procreant servant leaders, the question is, how do we produce them and place them in the neighborhoods and communities that need them? Peter Drucker has been credited with saying, "The best way to predict the future is to create it." In a spinoff, I believe that the best way to find servant leaders is to create them. Some may ask, "Is it practicable to recruit and train people to become procreant servant leaders?" For this question, I turn to the example of Jesus and his relationship with his twelve disciples. Jesus's model guides us from start to finish on how to find, transform, commission, and empower servant leaders who help themselves, help others, help others to help themselves, and create a spirit of generative servant leadership in the communities where they live and work. His model has stood the test of time for more than two thousand years and, today, is effectively used throughout the world.

The situation that happened in the first seven verses of Acts 6 gives a superb example of recognizing and promptly addressing a leadership problem by selecting, commissioning, and empowering procreant servant leaders who are prepared to lead. Interestingly, in the Acts 6 example, the procreant servant leaders had already been developed and had demonstrated a high level of career success, integrity, and administrative skills and were filled with the Holy Ghost. The job of the apostles and community of believers was to carefully select from among themselves men who were already prepared to lead, then commission and empower them to serve others and inspire servant leadership. Unfortunately, many of our communities may need to develop procreant servant leaders. In this case, we have the benefit of looking to the most reliable and time-tested model known to society, the relationship of Jesus and the eleven disciples who remained with him. This book has attempted to capture and publish the parameters of the procreant servant leadership development process as modeled by the life of Jesus in relationship with his disciples (mentees). The process is called **EDBI** (embracing, developing, building, and inspiring)**:**

- **Embracing** self-awareness and self-identity

- **Developing** biblically based character

- **Building** capacity to serve

- **Inspiring** others to serve

Beginning the Process – Learning our Language and Literature

A Story of a Gospel Singer
—Unknown

When my momma was pregnant with me, she went to church all the time, sang in the choir, and spent hours listening to gospel music, singing, and attending singings (concerts). She sang out loud to me and talk to me about God every day of her pregnancy. She would often say to me, "You will sing for the Lord one day."

After I was born, she sang to me every day, and as soon as I was able to utter words, she encouraged me to sing my name in a song. When I was two, she placed me in the Youth Day program at church to sing my first song, "Glory, Glory, Hallelujah." The church fell in love with me, and I have been singing ever since. Now, I am retiring after sixty years as a professional gospel singer.

This lady now talks passionately about finding herself in gospel music. She connects her life's story to her unborn and early childhood days, much of which she never knew about personally—yet she tells of her mother's pregnancy as though she was consciously observing. How does she know these things? How did they become such an inseparable part of her life's story?

....

Your story begins with others . . . How you were born? Where were you born? To whom you were born? All of these questions depend on the views of those who were there and able to remember. The point is that we must connect with others to learn our story. This is why our language and literature (story) is a great place to start.

Who's telling you your story? How do they know it? Who told them?

Following the Process – Carrying the M60

Ranger School is one of the US Army's premier leadership courses that trains soldiers and officers to work as a members of a team to accomplish a group mission under challenging physical and psychological conditions. What frightened Ranger Earl about this fifty-eight-day course more than anything else was the thought of not completing it the first time around. It was common knowledge that out of every class, there would be dropouts and students who would be recycled due to injuries or failure to meet the requirements. One way to fail the course or be recycled is by getting low peer ratings. After each of the four phases, peers rate one another, and those whose ratings are very low risk being recycled, which means having to redo a training phase—two more weeks of training in the same area.

Although Ranger Earl was in good physical condition compared to his peers, he had received low peer ratings in other training courses. But this time, Ranger Earl had devised a strategy that he hoped would keep him in good standing with his peers. His plan was to listen much more than he talked, be loyal to whomever was placed in charge, and volunteer for the tough jobs.

By far, the toughest and most unpopular job in a rifle platoon was carrying the M60 machine gun during patrols. The M60 machine gun is about 43.5 inches in length, with a forty-round interlinking ammunition belt. "The Pig" weighs around twenty-six pounds. Lifting and walking with "the Pig" for short distances was not a big deal, but carrying it on patrols for long distances was a grueling challenge that few people wanted to take on. Invariably, the platoon leader (PL) usually had to find a volunteer or assign a Ranger to carry the M60.

In the mountains of Dahlonega, Georgia, the PL yelled, "Who wants to carry the M60 for this mission?" as though it was a great honor to hump the thirty-pound weapon with ammunition. "One thousand one, one thousand two, one thousand three." The silence was suspenseful, and then an enthusiastic, "I'll carry it," responded Ranger Earl. Now with this assignment out of the way, the others were easy breezy. In fact, from that day on, Ranger Earl frequently volunteered to hump the Pig, except for the days that Ranger Earl was assigned other tasks by the ranger instructor, RI. On those days, others had to step up and carry the Pig.

Even though carrying the Pig long distances was a challenge, Ranger Earl soon developed a technique that made it appear as if it was as easy as carrying the M16 rifle. Although he had a pre-existing shoulder injury and flat foot problems that troubled him, Ranger Earl had learned how to carry the Pig in such a way that he avoided straining the tender part of his shoulder, and he carved out handmade arch supports for his feet. In short, he took care of his shoulder and feet so he could be ready to carry the Pig when called upon.

Amazingly, when Earl became the PL, most of his peers went out of their way to serve him, ensuring that his mission was successful and his peer evaluations were very high. Ranger Earl's willingness and consistency in serving others, quietly managing his own impediments and relying on the grace of God, made him a model team player in the eyes of his peers and RIs.

Although Ranger Earl did not know what servant leadership was, he had come to believe that serving others and helping them succeed was the best way to assure his own success. He discovered that caring for his own impediments and volunteering to help others succeed made him physically and mentally stronger and eventually made him a model of effective servant leadership for his peers. Ranger Earl is a real person and the author of this book.

Carrying an M60 introduced me to procreant servant leadership in the following ways:

- **Embracing self-awareness and self-identity:** I recognized my own impediments, wrapped them, and used them to help others.

- **Developing biblically based character:** I realized that helping others by genuinely serving a need, and doing it well, helped me to develop greater integrity and moral strength.

- **Building capacity to serve:** As I served others, my physical strength and fortitude grew, thereby expanding my ability and desire to serve in a greater capacity.

- **Inspiring others to serve:** My commitment to serving and encouraging others to serve inspired an attitude of service and gratitude in others.

Ending the Process – A Final Service Call

Servant leadership is a calling, and for some it may be a profession too. It grips us and often propels us to serve and inspire others up to our final days of life—as was so with the Supreme Model, Jesus, who from the cross at Calvary spoke words of healing and reaffirmation to many. His purpose called him to help others in his final moments of life. From the cross, he forgave a guilty man of his crimes and assured him a place in paradise, spoke blessings of forgiveness to those who belittled and denigrated him as he submitted himself in pain and agony to save them. He charged his brother to care for his mother as an example to others in caring for the at-risk and vulnerable, and finally, from the cross, he announced, "It is finished," signifying he had offered the ultimate sacrifice for sin: his life. He answered the final call for service from a publicly painful crucifixion.

The events of the crucifixion reveal two noteworthy observations about Jesus's final service call as a human.

First, it reveals that Jesus had a purpose-driven focus and second, he had an unconditional love for humanity.

1. **He had a purpose-driven focus:** Because Jesus sought to fulfill His God-given purpose, he endured the suffering and shame of the cross. His purpose-driven focus led him to the cross and kept him on the cross until the mission was achieved, for Jesus realized that there was no other way to achieve his God-given purpose. In the Garden of Gethsemane, he prayed, "Oh my father, if it be possible, let this cup pass from me, nevertheless, not my will, but thine be done." He prayed and acquiesced to the will of God.

2. **He had a deep love for humanity:** Although purpose pushed Jesus to the cross, his deep love for humanity caused him to minister to people while on the cross. This indiscriminate and unconditional agape love was on display as he helped and inspired hope in those who loved him, those who hated him, and those who were indifferent toward him.

Some might think it plausible that Jesus's suffering, bleeding, dying on the cross, and resurrection were enough to fulfill his ultimate purpose of securing salvation for humanity. Yet the suffering servant, in his final moments, while enduring excruciating pain and fighting for breath, as his lung may have collapsed against the weight of his body, took the opportunity to conduct his final acts of service before his death. Yes, he ministered from the cross to his mother and brother, spake words of forgiveness to his tormentors, and offered salvation to a dying thief, among other acts of service from the cross. In more recent history, during the final days of the life of Martin Luther King Jr., we observed his acts of procreant servant leadership. King shared in a speech about his call to go to Memphis, Tennessee, to help sanitation workers and their families fight for better wages and working conditions. During this time, King faced enormous challenges and mounting pressure to help people around the country. Some had even advised him not to go to Memphis because of the situation and the many death threats that were made on his life.

In his own voice, King talks about sitting on the runway in a plane with others as they awaited takeoff to Memphis. He said that the captain came over the public address system and apologized for the delayed flight departure and announced that Dr. Martin Luther King Jr. was on board and as a result, extra precautions had been taken to ensure that the baggage was properly checked and that the plane had been guarded all night. Additionally, King described during his Memphis speech that people warned him of many threats against his life. Even so, being tired and under great pressure and threats, King made his way to Memphis.

As he spoke to a crowd who had gathered to hear his instructions and inspiration, he spoke about the Good Samaritan. From the parable about the Good Samaritan, King described a man who lay helpless on the ground while both a priest and Levite passed by without helping. King suggested that there may have been many reasons why neither of the men stopped to help, but it all came down to the question of self-concern: what would happen to them if they stopped to help this desperate man?
King then told the response of the Good Samaritan who came by, stopped, helped the man, and invested in his full recovery. King went on to say that perhaps the Samaritan reversed the question and asked not, "What will happen to me if I stop to help this man?" but, "What will happen to me if I do not stop and help him?"

In his final hours and final speech, King said that he had come to Memphis because he was concerned about what would happen to the hundreds of sanitation workers and their families if the citizens of Memphis didn't stop to help them.

This was King's final opportunity to serve others and inspire them to help one another. Perhaps this was his final public service call to lift others as he fulfilled his own purpose for living. The next day, following his Memphis speech, King was killed by an assassin.

As you face the pressing challenges of today and tomorrow and as you seek to do God's will, you must stand with a deep resolve to ask not "What will happen to me if I help the indigent?" but, "What will happen him if I do not stop and help him?"

If I Don't Stop to Help, What Will Happen to Him?

If I don't help the wounded,

what will happen to him?

His children,

His family,

His heritage

His hopes and dreams

His connectivity to God.

If I don't help the indigent

who will help develop her character?

Befriend,

Shape,

Mold,

Disciple, and

Indoctrinate him

If I don't help the underprepared,

who will build her capacity?

Sharpen, expand, and polish her skills and talents

Teach critical thinking

Promote positivity

Challenge mediocrity and

Lead by example

If I don't impart passion and purpose,
Who will inspire and empower?
Share mission
Project purpose
Commission to duty and
Impart power

If I don't lift and lead,
who will?
The wealthy
The famous
The needy
The misguided

If I don't stop to help, who will?

References

Blanchard, Kenneth. *Servant Leadership in Action: How You Can Achieve Great Relationships and Results.* 2018.

Degruy, Joy. *Post Traumatic Slave Syndrome.* Upton Press, 2005.

Eckel, Mark. "I Just Need Time to Think! Reflective Study as Christian Practice." 2013. https://www.amazon.com/Just-Need-Time-Think-Reflective/dp/149081938X/ref=asap_bc?ie=UTF8.

Gilchrist, P. R. *Theological Workbook of the Old Testament.* Chicago: Moody, 1980.

Greenleaf, Robert. "The Institution as Servant." Seton Hall University, Presidents Hall 4A, 400 South Orange Avenue, South Orange, NJ 07079.

Greenleaf, Robert. "The Servant as Leader." Seton Hall University, Presidents Hall 4A, 400 South Orange Avenue, South Orange, NJ 07079.

Hackett, Conrad, and David McClendon. "Christians Remain World's Largest Religious Group, But They Are Declining in Europe." *Pew Research Center*, 2017. https://www.pewresearch.org/fact-tank/2017/04/05/christians-remain-worlds-largest-religious-group-but-they-are-declining-in-europe/.

Hamilton, Adam. "Why Nazareth?" *Ministry Matters*, July 25, 2011. https://www.ministrymatters.com/all/entry/1469/why-nazareth.

Indeed Editorial Team. "What Is Servant Leadership? 10 Principles of Servant Leadership." *Indeed*, June 18, 2021. https://www.indeed.com/career-advice/career-development/servant-leadership#:~:text=Servant%20leadership%20is%20a%20management%20style%20in%20which,produce%20higher%20quality%20work%20more%20efficiently%20and%20productively.

King, Jr., Martin Luther. "I've Been to the Mountain Top Speech." *AFSCME*, 1968. https://www.afscme.org/about/history/mlk/mountaintop.

M60 Machine Gun. https://machinegunamericaorlando.com/gun/m60/.

Nouwen, Henri J. M. *The Wounded Healer.* New York, NY: Doubleday, 1979.

"Praxis." *Wikipedia*, https://en.wikipedia.org/wiki/Praxis_(process).

Rohn, John. "It Only Takes 6 Steps to Plan Your Success." *Success*, 2015. https://www.success.com/author/jim-rohn.

The National Society of Leadership and Success. https://www.nsls.org/.

Washington, Booker T. *Character Building*. Speeches compiled and given at Tuskegee Normal and Industrial Institute. *Project Gutenberg*. https://www.gutenberg.org/ebooks/60484.

Wilkes, C. Jean. *Life Way Press*. One LifeWay Plaza, Nashville, TN, 1996.

All Scriptural references are taken from the Holy Bible, New International Version, unless otherwise noted. Some of the references used in this book are listed below.
1. Acts 1:4-8
2. Acts 2: 1 & 4 & 14
3. 2 Cor. twelve:7-10
4. Matthew 28:18-20
5. Matthew 20:25-27
6. Luke 3:23
7. Luke 4:18
8. Matthew 4:23-25

9. Matthew 20:25-28.
10. Matthew 25:14 – 30
11. Matthew 16:19-20,
12. Luke 6:twelve-16.
13. Luke 2:42
14. Luke 2:52
15. Acts 5:33
16. Acts 5:34-39
17. Luke 10:25-37
18. John 17:twelve
19. John 2:13-18
20. Psalm 69:9
21. Romans 11:18
22. Genesis 1:26-27
23. Acts 2:1-4
24. Acts 13:2-3
25. Acts 6:7
26. Luke 4:18-19
27. Luke 4
28. Mark 14:3-9
29. Mark 14:6-9
30. Revelations 21-22
31. Luke 5:1-10
32. 2 Samuel 7:8-9
33. 2 Timothy 3:16-17
34. James 3:1
35. Mathew 22:39
36. Ecclesiastes 3:1
37. Psalms twelve1:4

STANFORD E. ANGION

Stanford Angion was born in Coy Alabama, to Rosetta Angion a single parent. He joined Mt. Gilead Baptist Church in Coy, Alabama, as a young boy. In fall 1982, he attended Alabama A&M University, where he graduated with a Bachelor's degree in Soil Science and received an active-duty commission into the United States Army as a Second Lieutenant. Angion graduated from Alabama A&M University in December 1986 and began his active-duty military service in August 1987. He spent 13 years in the United States Army and attained the rank of major. In 1999, Angion accepted his call into the gospel ministry to preach and was honorably discharged from the Army in October 2000.

February 4, 1995, Angion was married to Athenia Marie Hudson from Cleveland, Ohio. They met and married in Oahu, Hawaii. Two daughters were born to this union, Ivana and Kendra. Both are graduates of Alabama State University, teach in the Montgomery

Public School System.

Angion was licensed as a baptist preacher in March 2000 and ordained later that year. He served as Youth Pastor for two years at Mt. Zion Baptist Church in Hinesville, GA, under the leadership of Rev. M.L. Jackson. In July 2003, he was installed as pastor of Mt. Gilead Missionary Baptist Church in Coy, AL, where he presently serves. Under his leadership, the congregation has built a Family Recreational Park, renovated the sanctuary, and started MGS&A Institute. The Institute offers a variety of programs and courses designed to train students in the performing arts and enhance elementary and secondary student learning.

As a sophomore at Alabama A & M University, Angion became a member of the Phi Beta Sigma Fraternity, Incorporated and is presently an active member of the Alpha Eta Sigma Chapter in Montgomery.

Angion's educational accomplishments include a Bachelor of Soil Science from Alabama A&M University in Huntsville, AL; a Master's of Journalism and Mass Communications, from Marshall University in Huntington, WV; a Master's of Education, from the University of West Alabama; a Master's of Arts in Bible and Pastoral Ministry, from Selma University; and a Doctor of Education from Alabama State University in Montgomery, AL. In November 2003, Angion published a book, Unleashing the Inner Strength of Youth; Nov. 2014 he published Invigorating Hope; and July 2015, he published an Implementation Guide for Invigorating Hope.

On August 1, 2016, Angion assumed responsibilities as the Vice President for Academic Affairs at Selma University. In June 2020, he was assigned to the position of Provost/Vice President, a capacity in which he served until appointed as the Interim President at Selma University. He served a as interim President at Selma University from February 12 to April 19, 2021, and was appointed as the 25th President of Selma University on April 19, 2021, where he presently serves.

Made in the USA
Columbia, SC
20 October 2024